PowerPoint

FOR BUSY PEOPLE

PowerPoint
FOR BUSY PEOPLE

Ron Mansfield

Osborne/**McGraw-Hill**

Berkeley / New York / St. Louis / San Francisco / Auckland / Bogotá
Hamburg / London / Madrid / Mexico City / Milan / Montreal / New Delhi
Panama City / Paris / São Paulo / Singapore / Sydney / Tokyo / Toronto

Osborne/**McGraw-Hill**
2600 Tenth Street
Berkeley, California 94710
U.S.A.

For information on translations or book distributors outside the U.S.A., or to arrange bulk purchase discounts for sales promotions, premiums, or fundraisers, please contact Osborne **McGraw-Hill** at the above address.

PowerPoint for Busy People

1234567890 DOC 99876

ISBN 0-07-882204-1

Acquisitions Editor: Joanne Cuthbertson
Project Editor: Claire Splan
Copy Editor: Daniel Lewis
Proofreader: Pat Mannion
Indexer: Valerie Robbins
Computer Designers: Roberta Steele, Leslee Bassin
Quality Control: Joe Scuderi
Series and Cover Designer: Ted Mader Associates
Series Illustrator: Daniel Barbeau

To Grandpa Lee

About the Author

Ron Mansfield is a microcomputer consultant and author of *Windows 95 for Busy People, Excel for Windows 95 for Busy People*, and *Working in Microsoft Office* (Osborne/McGraw-Hill). He has also written best-selling books on Microsoft Word for Windows and DOS 6.2. Mansfield is a frequent lecturer at national computer and writers seminars and has written hundreds of articles for industry magazines and newsletters.

Contents at a glance

Contents

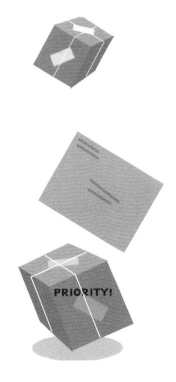

Acknowledgments

Gee, I love working with Osborne/McGraw-Hill! This was as painless a book as I can remember. The only frustrating thing is that there are many hard-working and talented OMH workers that I still haven't met. Looks like it is time for another trip to Berkeley.

Many thanks, of course, to acquisitions editor Joanne Cuthbertson She is always a delight to work with and a constant source of sunshine. If you've read other books in the Busy People series, you have probably guessed that Ted Mader, Mary Jo Kovarik, and Marla Shelasky are all responsible for this book's wonderful design. Dan Barbeau created the various creatures found wandering through the pages (and, I suspect, the matching tee shirts, and the coffee mugs, and who knows what else).

The mind-boggling task of project management fell to Claire Splan, who was so spent at the end of this project that she was forced to fly to Paris, France for three weeks to recuperate. I'm telling you, publishing is hell. Associate editor Heidi Poulin kept us all in line as usual, keeping track of all the things we lost, and covering our collective butts. Our talented copy editor Dan Lewis made sure that I didn't break too many rules—no small task, I assure you. Eagle-eyed Pat Mannion was the last person to weed out typos, something we're all grateful for. Thanks also to the exhaustive efforts of the production team, including Roberta Steele, Leslee Bassin, Richard Whitaker, Lance Ravella, and Peter Hancik. These are the folks who really make ideas actually become books.

In management, we have executive editor Scott Rogers to thank for his undying belief in the Busy People series, and his tireless effort to see that the word gets out. Controller Katharine Johnson and marketing manager Kendal Andersen were also crucial to the successful launch of this series.

None of this would mean much if you didn't buy the books, and you can't purchase what stores don't stock. The reason that you are holding this book now is that a dedicated crew of sales folks and your local bookseller all got excited about the project too. Thank you, one and all.

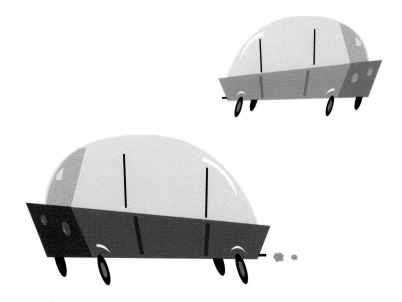

Introduction

When Osborne/McGraw-Hill approached me about their new *Busy People* series, I couldn't wait to get started! The publisher was looking for authors who understand that many readers have only a night or a few lunch hours to learn a new software package. Certainly the digital revolution has empowered us, but it has also accelerated everyone's expectations. How often do people say to you things like "We need you in Atlanta tomorrow to explain the new product line to the regional reps," or "Can you put together a marketing presentation for this hot new prospect we have found? Their VPs are visiting the plant this Tuesday," or "I'm swamped. Can you put together the slides for Friday's board meeting?"

To meet these needs, the editors expected opinionated, thoughtfully organized writing with a touch of skepticism. Fat-free fun. It was a perfect match. I hope you enjoy reading this book at least as much as I enjoyed writing it.

I KNOW YOU'RE IN A HURRY, SO...

Let's cut to the chase. If you haven't yet installed PowerPoint, do that now. If you need help, check out the instructions that came with PowerPoint or Microsoft Office.

Once you have PowerPoint up and running, I suggest cruising Chapter 1 and reading Chapter 2 first, but you'll be fine no matter how much you bounce around. In a remarkably short period of time, you'll be able to:

- Start and quit PowerPoint
- Create, rehearse, and give great presentations

- Get online help
- Use and create templates for repetitive tasks like quarterly meetings
- Rearrange and reformat presentations
- Deal with printing and font issues
- Use PowerPoint's built-in outlines for "everyday" meetings
- Include multimedia elements like movies in your presentations
- Create 35mm slides, overhead transparencies, and paper handouts
- Create self-running video slide presentations for trade shows
- Share presentations and collaborate with co-workers
- Personalize the look, feel, and sound of PowerPoint

Remember, though: just because you *can* do something with PowerPoint doesn't mean that you *should*. Simple is often best, particularly when you are busy. I'll try to remind you of that from time to time throughout the book.

POWERPOINT 95: THE NEXT GENERATION

If you've used earlier versions of PowerPoint, you'll appreciate this next step in the evolutionary process. PowerPoint 95 is Windows 95 savvy, which is to say it can use long filenames, sports new easier-to-use Open and Save boxes, and much more.

You'll also appreciate the new Answer Wizard, a powerful Help feature, and AutoClipArt, a system that scans your presentation text looking for key words and suggesting illustrations you can add to slides. As you will soon learn, there are other improvements too, like multiple undos, additional meeting support, and much more.

Microsoft says it is moving towards a time when we will all think more about our *data* and less about specific, name-brand *programs* used to create them. The lines are already blurring when we employ tools like object linking and embedding (OLE). If you believe the

Microsoft public relations blitz, one day you'll forget about Microsoft Word and Excel and PowerPoint and just assemble menus of your favorite data-manipulating commands. Naturally, Microsoft will be selling us these tools, or perhaps building them into Windows 99. There are many miles to go before this becomes a reality, if ever. But in any case, I'll point out a few of the signposts for these new directions and try to get you into the habit of thinking about documents and tasks rather than just about programs.

Most of this is accomplished without sacrificing performance. In fact, many things (like printing) usually happen faster now, thanks to 32-bit support and other Windows 95 advancements.

THINGS YOU MIGHT WANT TO KNOW ABOUT THIS BOOK

You can read this book more or less in any order. Use the book as a reference, or read it cover-to-cover. Here's a quick run down of the important elements you'll encounter as you go:

Fast Forward

Each chapter begins with a section called *Fast Forward*. These sections should always be your first stop if you are a confident user, or impatient, or habitually late. You should find everything you need to get back on stride. Think of them as the *Reader's Digest* version of each chapter. This shorthand may leave you hungry, especially if you are new to Windows or PowerPoint, so for more complete and leisurely explanations of techniques and shortcuts, read the rest of the chapter.

Fast Forwards are, in effect, a book within a book—a built-in quick reference guide summarizing the key tasks explained in each chapter. Written step by step, point by point, Fast Forwards also include illustrations and page references to guide you to the more complete information presented in the chapter.

Habits & Strategies

Don't overlook the *Habits* & *Strategies* margin notes. These short paragraphs suggest

Throughout the book, cross-references and other minor asides appear in the margin notes like this one.

timesaving tips, techniques, and worthwhile addictions. (I've included them because, as Mark Twain once said, "Nothing so needs reforming as other people's habits.")

These habits and strategies also give you the big picture and help you plan ahead. For example, the long filenames you can use in Windows 95 and PowerPoint are great, but they cause some interesting problems if you share files with users of Windows 3.1 or earlier PowerPoint versions. So I've included some suggested file-naming strategies.

Shortcuts

Shortcuts are designed with the busy person in mind. When there's a way to do something that may not be as fancy as the material in the text, but is *faster*, it will be described in the margin and high-lighted by the special Shortcut icon.

Cautions

Sometimes it's just too easy to plunge ahead, fall down a rabbit hole, and spend hours of extra time finding your way back to where you were before you went astray. This hard hat will warn you before you commit potentially time-consuming mistakes.

Definitions

Usually, I'll explain computer jargon in the text when the techno-babble first occurs. But occasionally, you'll see this body builder icon in the margin. Most of the time these definitions are informal and often a little playful.

Upgrade Notes

If you've used earlier versions of PowerPoint, be on the look-out for *upgrade notes*. They will tell you when something has changed and make sure you don't miss any of the latest advances.

Menu Selection Shortcut

Finally, I should mention a navigational shortcut I've adopted for menu commands. Occasionally I use a shorthand writing style that employs a "stick" to separate each choice in a menu selection sequence. So, for example, when describing the process of printing, I'll say "Choose File|Print" instead of "Choose the Print command from the File menu."

LET'S DO IT!

Ready? Hang out the Do Not Disturb sign, open that Jolt cola, and let's dig into PowerPoint 95 before PowerPoint 96 arrives!

Incidentally, I'm always happy to hear your reactions to this or any of my other books. You can reach me through the publisher, or on the Net (**rmansfield@aol.com**).

The Basics

1

FAST FORWARD

START POWERPOINT ➤ *pp. 9-10*
- Choose PowerPoint from the Start menu (look in the Office submenu, perhaps), or
- Double-click a PowerPoint presentation file icon, or
- Use the Office Toolbar.

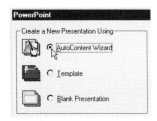

CREATE NEW PRESENTATIONS ➤ *pp. 10-11, 17-20*
- Choose one of the three Create a New Presentation choices in the PowerPoint "greeting" screen, or
- Choose New from the File menu, or
- In the Office toolbar choose Start a New Document, then select a presentation type in the resulting New dialog box.
- In any case, you can use predefined presentations and designs or create your own.
- Click in a text box to enter and edit text.
- Double-click in boxes designed to hold graphic elements to add them.

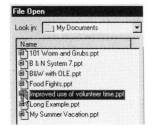

OPEN EXISTING PRESENTATIONS ➤ *pp. 22-24*
- Double-click presentation file icons in Windows windows (My Computer or Explorer windows, for example) or dialog boxes, or
- Pick from the last five files you've used (listed on the PowerPoint File menu), or
- Use the Open command on the PowerPoint File menu or Office toolbar.
- You might also check the Start menu's Documents submenu for recently used PowerPoint files.

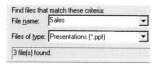

USE FIND TO LOCATE PRESENTATIONS ➤ *pp. 24-25*

1. Choose Open from the File menu.
2. Specify a place to look (a folder or disk) in the Look in list.
3. Type a complete or partial filename in the Filename box.
4. Click Advanced and make sure Search subfolders is checked.
5. Click the Find Now button.
6. When the icon for the desired file appears in the resulting list, double-click to use it.

PREVIEW PRESENTATIONS IN THE OPEN DIALOG BOX ➤ *pp. 22-23*

1. Select the file of interest in the File Open dialog box's scrolling list.
2. A preview of the first page of the specified presentation file should appear in the preview box.

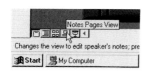

SWITCH VIEWS ➤ *p. 12*

- Switch views by clicking the appropriate view buttons in the bottom-left corner of the PowerPoint window.
- Matching view options are available in the View menu.

SAVE PRESENTATIONS ➤ *p. 20*

1. Choose Save from the File menu, or use the CTRL-S shortcut.
2. Specify a folder location using the Save in box.
3. Type a filename in the File name box. (PowerPoint will add the .ppt extension for you.)
4. Click the Save button or press ENTER.
   Use the Save as type command to save a previously stored file under a different name or in a different location. You can also use the Save button (looks like a diskette) in the Standard toolbar.

VIEW A PRESENTATION ONSCREEN ➤ *pp. 20-21*

1. Open the presentation
2. Click the Slide Show button at the lower-left corner of the PowerPoint window.
3. If you see a slide other than the first one, hold down both mouse buttons for two seconds and release them to go to the first slide.
4. Press the left (primary) mouse button to advance slides or use RIGHT ARROW and LEFT ARROW keys to move forward and backward. You can also use the PAGE UP and PAGE DOWN keys.

PRINT SLIDES ➤ *pp. 21-22*

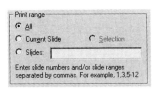

1. Choose Print from the File menu.
2. Specify the desired printer if you have more than one.
3. Make sure Slides is displayed in the Print what section of the dialog box.
4. Specify a range of slides to print (All, Current Slide, and so forth).
5. Specify the desired number of copies and how you want them collated.
6. Make sure your printer is ready.
7. Click OK.

PRINT HANDOUTS ➤ *pp. 21-22*

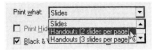

1. Choose Print from the File menu.
2. Specify the desired printer if you have more than one.
3. Make sure "Handouts" (2, 3, or 6 slides per page) is displayed in the Print what section of the dialog box.
4. Specify a range of handouts to print (All, Current slide, and so forth).
5. Specify the desired number of copies and how you want them collated.
6. Make sure your printer is ready.
7. Click OK.

QUIT POWERPOINT ➤ *p. 25*

1. Choose Exit from the File menu.
2. You will be prompted to save or discard any unsaved changes.

Do you remember when you could stand up, say what was on your mind, deal with the audience reaction and sit down? I do. For those of you too young to recall, back then we used a china marker and a white board, or a giant flip pad on an easel, or bar napkins.

But it's a jungle out there now. And survivors are using more potent weapons. Your audience expects to be dazzled. They want to see color, motion, and special effects. To a large extent, *how* a presentation looks is often as important as what it says.

PowerPoint will help you create good-looking overhead transparencies, 35mm slides, and even video slide shows. And while it is true that most of what PowerPoint does can also be done by Word or Excel or a drawing program, PowerPoint streamlines many presentation tasks, and provides some excellent prefabricated layouts, color schemes, and font choices. Let's take a look.

BUZZWORDS

Anything worth learning requires the acquisition of a few new buzzwords, and PowerPoint, while it is extremely straightforward, is no exception. It's worth spending a couple of minutes to get the jargon down.

Slides

You create and edit individual pages called *slides*. For instance, in a sales presentation you might have a slide titled Competition, another called Pricing, and so on. Here are four typical PowerPoint slides.

These "pages" are called slides even if you never convert them to 35mm slides.

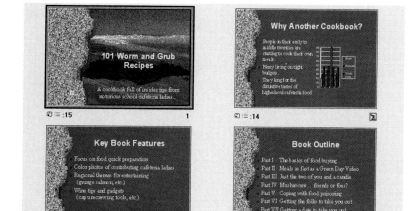

Speaker's Notes

Use speaker's notes when you present. They are usually printed on paper and can be either the exact text of the speech, reminder notes, back-up information, or combinations thereof. Here is an example of speaker's notes.

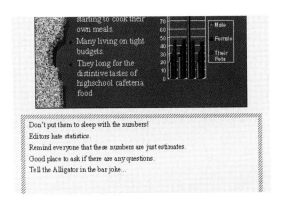

Handouts

Handouts are paper copies of all or some of the slides to be given to the audience. They can be one per page or reduced so that two, three, or six fit on a sheet of paper. Figure 1.1 shows a typical handout. Notice how PowerPoint will place up to six slides on a single sheet of paper.

Presentation Files

All of the PowerPoint slides for a particular project (a sales presentation, for instance) are kept in a single PowerPoint file called a *presentation file*. These presentation files normally end with the extension .ppt (**Sales.ppt**, for example).

A presentation file might have just a few slides or many. If you've recorded sounds as part of your presentation or added speaker's notes, or added a video clip, those presentation elements will also be stored in the presentation file. In other words, a typical presentation consists of only one file, making it easy to copy and pass around presentations. (Unless, of course you've used OLE to link your presentation with other files as discussed in Chapter 6.)

Depending upon your Windows 95 settings, you might not see the .ppt extensions at the end of filenames, but PowerPoint will show you (in the Open and Save dialog boxes) all files it thinks are PowerPoint presentation files based on their extensions. (It will list all .ppt files.)

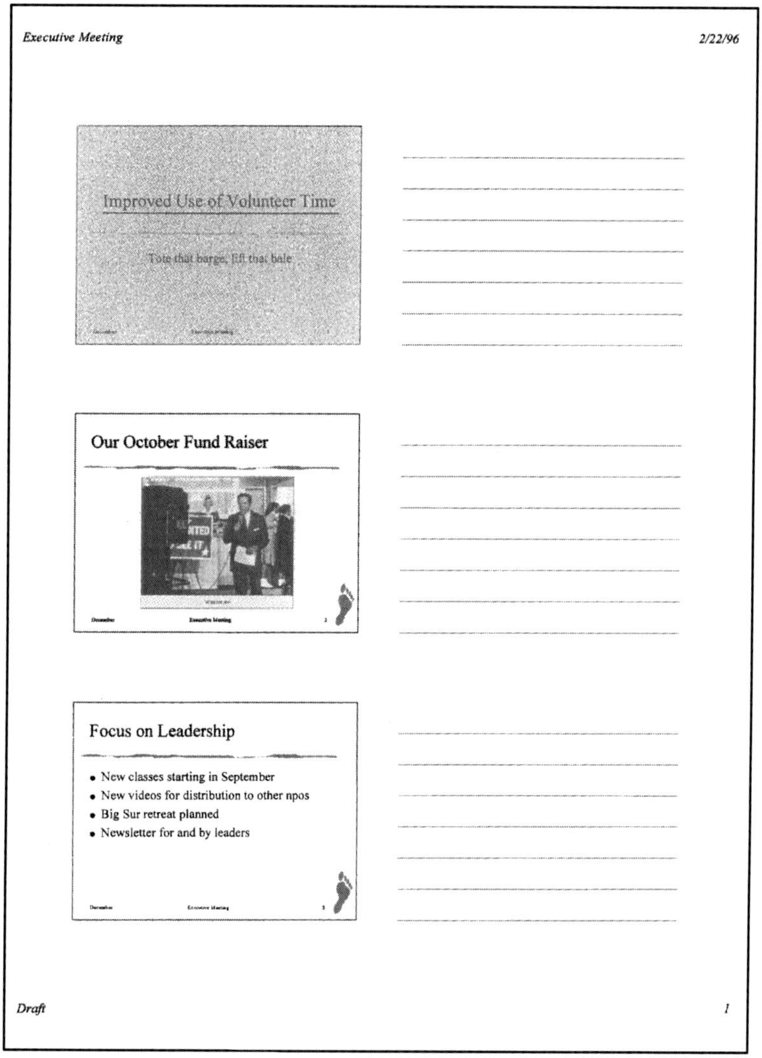

Figure 1.1 Print handouts for your audience and perhaps for yourself.

Masters

You create *masters* (also called *master slides*) to hold information that will appear on multiple slides in your presentation. For instance, if you wanted to put your name, company logo, or some other decoration on each slide, you'd add it to the master for that presentation.

You can also create separate masters for handouts and speaker's notes within each presentation. PowerPoint comes with a variety of preprogrammed masters to get you started. You can use these as is, modify them, or create your own masters from scratch. Here is one master, designed to make it easy to create slides with bulleted lists. Notice how it has a line containing a bullet.

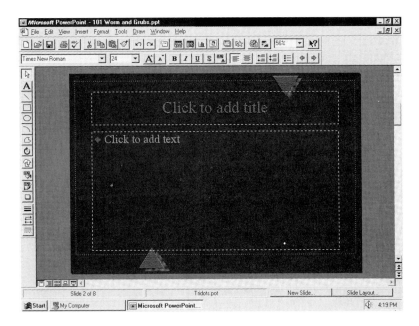

PREDEFINED COLOR SCHEMES

PowerPoint lets you define rules used for applying colors or shades of gray to the various components of your presentation. For instance, you can specify a slide's background colors, the colors used for major headings, and so on. PowerPoint comes with many predefined color schemes, which you can use as is or modify to taste. Chapter 5 explores colors and shades of gray in more detail.

POWERPOINT TEMPLATES

A PowerPoint *template* consists of a master and a color scheme. PowerPoint comes with as many as 160 predefined templates (depending upon how you installed PowerPoint). For example, this slide was created with a template that includes a diamond-shaped graphic and changes the colors of headings and bullets.

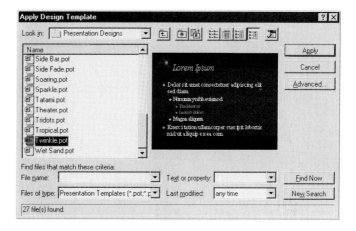

If you've created presentations containing your own custom masters and color schemes, you can use these as templates. To change the *look* of a presentation, you need merely apply a different template to an existing presentation to completely change the presentation's appearance. PowerPoint makes all the necessary changes in colors, fonts, and so on. (You'll see how this all works in Chapter 4.)

GETTING STARTED

"All right, Mansfield, enuff minutiae. We're busy people. Let's make some slides, already." Start PowerPoint as you would any other Office program. One way is to choose PowerPoint from the Windows 95 Start menu. It will be on the Programs submenu, either out there on its own, or perhaps in the Microsoft Office submenu.

As always, you can double-click the program icon or a document icon in Windows Explorer instead. You can also click the Start a New Document or Open a Document button, in the Office shortcut bar shown here:

Tip of the Day at Startup

Unless you turn this feature off, you will be greeted with a PowerPoint *Tip of the Day*. The tips are all worth reading at least once, but when you know them by heart, it's perfectly okay to remove the checkmark from the Show Tips at Startup box in the Tip of the Day window, you power user, you. This will prevent tips from showing at startup.

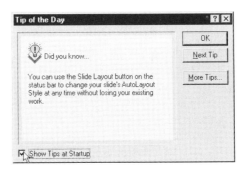

Choosing to Create a New Presentation or Use an Existing One

When you dismiss the Tip dialog box by clicking on the OK button, you will see a second dialog box simply titled PowerPoint:

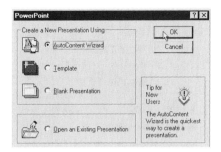

It wants to know if you'd like to create a new presentation or work with an existing one. Notice that, if creating a new presentation, you have the options of using several wizards and template choices. We'll take a quick look at these choices in a moment, and in Chapters 3 and 4 will explore them in detail.

THE POWERPOINT WORKSPACE

As you can see in Figure 1.2, PowerPoint will remind you of other Windows 95 programs. There is a "parent window" and one or more

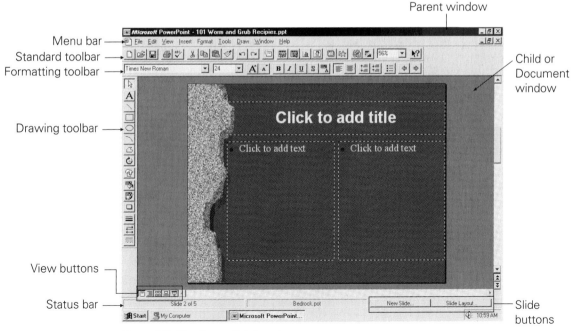

Figure 1.2 The PowerPoint workspace.

"child windows" containing presentations. You'll find the usual assortment of scrolling tools and window control boxes (for sizing, minimizing, and closing windows).

VIEWS

Like other Microsoft Office products, PowerPoint offers different views for entering, editing, and previewing your information. For instance, PowerPoint's Outline view is handy for entering text and for rearranging the text in a given slide, but once you've done the bulk of the typing, you'll want to switch to other PowerPoint views. They include:

- Slide view
- Slide Sorter view
- Notes Pages view
- Slide Show view

Switching Views

You can switch views by using the View menu or the view buttons (shown below) at the bottom-left of the PowerPoint window. The buttons are named (from left to right) Slide View, Outline View, Slide Sorter View, Notes Pages View, and Slide Show View.

Outline View

It's easy to rearrange the topic and subtopic items while in Outline view. And you can collapse items in this view to see just headings or just the names of each slide. For example, to show just the title for each slide you could use the Show Titles button. You work with outline buttons in much the same way you do in Word's Outline view. Chapter 3 has the details.

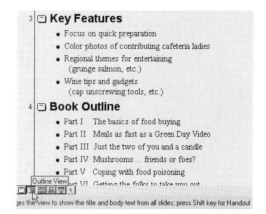

Slide View

Slide view shows you how your finished slides will look. You'll see the backgrounds, colors or shades of gray, and so forth. Here is a typical slide in Slide view.

You can move from slide to slide with the PAGE UP and PAGE DOWN keys, the scroll box, or the paging buttons located below the scroll bar.

You can edit text and other slide elements while in Slide view, as you will learn in Chapter 4.

Slide Sorter View

The Slide Sorter view allows you to see "thumbnails" such as those shown here.

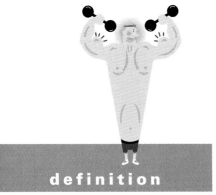

Thumbnails: *Small reproductions of PowerPoint slides, particularly useful when rearranging presentations or printing handouts. See also Optometry.*

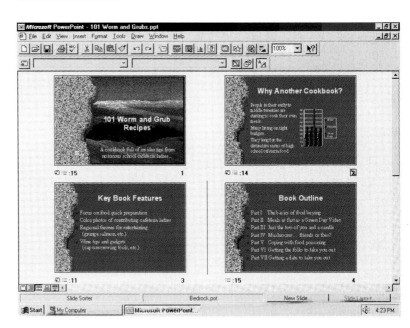

While in Slide Sorter view you can drag slides to move them. Chapter 3 shows how to do this. The Slide Sorter view is also where you specify types of slide transitions. For example, you can make one slide dissolve into another or make slides appear and disappear using Venetian blind effects. You can also specify how individual bullet points on a slide are revealed to the audience (all at once or one at a time). Slide Sorter is an excellent view to use for this purpose because you get a preview of the effects as you choose them.

Notes Pages View

Use the Notes Pages view to create and see notes to the presenter. It shows a miniature slide image and provides a text area for presenter's notes.

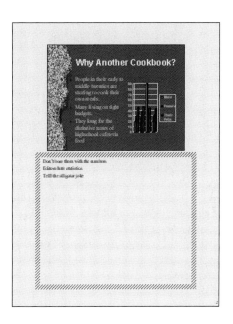

SHORTCUT

Use the View menu's Zoom command to make the notes readable.

To enter a note:

1. Click in the text area beneath the slide. The box outline will change appearance.
2. Type and edit in the note box as you would in any other.

As you will see in Chapter 9, you can print these notes if you like.

Slide Show View

Use Slide Show view to help you rehearse, or for actual video presentations of finished shows. It removes all of the PowerPoint screen clutter and places a small icon in the lower-left corner of the screen, as shown in the following illustration.

MY SUMMER VACATION

NOTES FROM A MEXICAN
PRISON CELL

When you switch to Slide Show view, you'll see the slide you were working on in the previous view. To move forward (to see higher numbered slides), either press the SPACEBAR, click the primary mouse button, or use the RIGHT ARROW key. Use the LEFT ARROW key to move backwards.

If you click on the little icon, a menu will pop up with a multitude of helpful options. Among other things, you can opt to have a "pen" at your disposal. Using the mouse to write with this pen, you can draw temporary lines on the screen, emphasizing things as you talk. These lines are not saved with the presentation, and might remind you of chalk marks—visible only during the current presentation or rehearsal.

You can also use this menu to change the color of the pen, to go to a particular slide, or to make the screen black.

To leave the Slide Show view, press ESC or choose End Show from the pop-up menu. You'll be switched to the previous view you were using. You'll learn more about slide shows in Chapters 7 and 11.

SHORTCUT

You can see the shortcut menu at any time by right-clicking. This is handy if you've chosen to hide the icon (which you do from the pop-up menu).

Black and White View

Black and White view converts color presentations into black and white so you can see how they will look and print in monochrome. A miniature color slide will appear as well:

CREATING PRESENTATIONS THE EASY WAY

It's the wizards, templates, layouts, and masters that put the *power* in PowerPoint. While you *could* format each slide manually, the combination of wizardry automation and predesigned layouts greatly simplifies the task. There's even a wizard called *AutoContent* that will help you develop a presentation's content and organization. So let's get off on the right foot by looking at automation first. (This is just a tease. You'll learn about manual techniques, and more about sorcerers—er, I mean *Wizard*—in later chapters.)

upgrade note

This AutoContent Wizard is pretty slick. It asks you for a meeting topic, then provides a proposed meeting outline. All you need to do is add the specifics, and perhaps rearrange or delete things. Check it out.

QUICKLY CREATING YOUR FIRST PRESENTATION

Perhaps the quickest way to create a presentation is to use the AutoContent Wizard. Suppose, for instance, that you wanted to create a presentation to outline your progress on a recent work assignment. You elicit the help of the wizard either by choosing the AutoContent Wizard on the PowerPoint "greeting" screen, or by choosing New from the File menu, and then double-clicking the AutoContent Wizard icon in the Presentations tab.

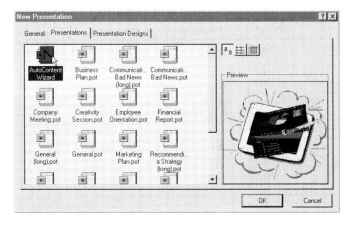

In either case you will be greeted by a wizard with seemingly endless questions. Read the screens carefully and answer queries as they arise. Use the Next and Back buttons to navigate.

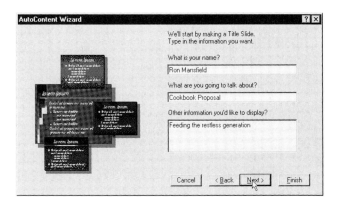

One of the fascinating things about the AutoContent Wizard is its ability to provide outlines for common meeting tasks. For example, here's an outline for progress reporting:

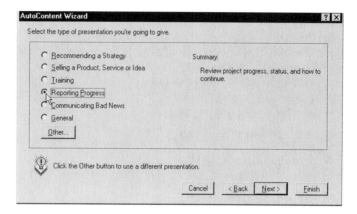

You are even asked how long you'd like to stand in front of the audience during your presentation:

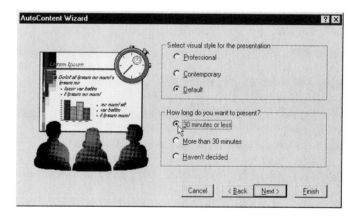

When the wizard has her answers, she creates the shell of a presentation to which you add your own words (again, we'll go into detail later). Basically, you click in a text box to enter or edit text, or double-click design elements to add graphs, insert photos, and so on:

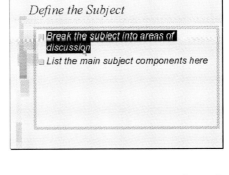

habits & strategies

I like to save whenever I've finished a complex, time-consuming task or every 15 minutes, whichever comes first. I also save whenever the phone rings, or when I am otherwise interrupted.

Although PowerPoint for Windows 95 supports long filenames, consider using filenames of eight or fewer characters if you exchange your work with users of earlier Windows or PowerPoint versions.

SAVING PRESENTATIONS

It's a good idea to save presentations regularly as you work. Either use the Save command on the File menu or the Save button on the Standard toolbar. The CTRL-S keyboard shortcut also works here. PowerPoint's inclination is to save your work in a folder called My Documents, usually located on your C: drive. You can tell Power-Point to save your work elsewhere if you like by using the *Save in* list in the File Save dialog box:

To save a previously saved presentation under a different name (or in a different location) use the *Save as* command instead.

VIEWING A PRESENTATION

The process of viewing presentations is a chapter unto itself (Chapter 11, in fact). But here's a taste:

1. Click the Slide Show button.
2. All of the PowerPoint controls and menus will disappear. You'll see a full screen representation of one of your slides.
3. If it's not the first slide and you want to start at the very beginning, hold down both mouse buttons for two seconds and release them.
4. To advance to the next slide click the left (the primary) mouse button.
5. You can also use the RIGHT ARROW and LEFT ARROW keys to move forward and back.
6. Right-clicking reveals a handy pop-up menu full of navigational choices and presentation tools (discussed in Chapter 11).

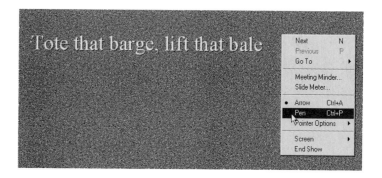

7. To leave Slide view, press ESC.

PRINTING BASICS

You can print slides and other handouts with the Print command found on the File menu. The command presents you with a Print dialog box, shown in the following illustration, where you specify the printer you wish to use, the number of copies desired, the range of items to be printed, and so forth. This is also where you tell PowerPoint if you want to print slides, handouts, and so on. Learn more about printing in Chapter 9.

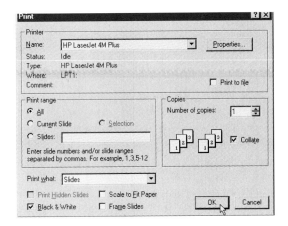

OPENING EXISTING PRESENTATIONS AT STARTUP

To open an existing presentation (one you or someone else has previously created), click the Open an Existing Presentation option, then click OK or press ENTER.

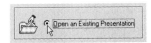

You might be presented with a list of PowerPoint presentations in a File Open dialog box:

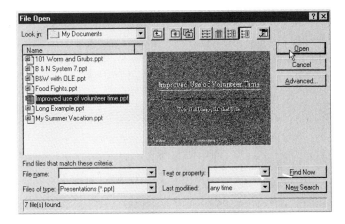

Click once on a presentation's name in the Name list to see a preview of the presentation (actually the first slide). To work with a listed presentation, simply double-click its name in the Name list, or click the name once and then click the Open button, if that's your preference.

OPENING EXISTING PRESENTATIONS AFTER STARTUP

Frequently, the quickest way to open a recently used presentation is to pick its name from the File list.

If the desired file is not listed use the File menu's Open command instead.

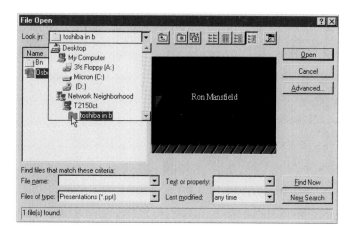

1. Choose Open from the File menu.

*By default, PowerPoint saves
your work in the My Documents
folder on your primary hard disk
(usually C:). It's always a good
place to look first.*

2. Specify a disk or folder with the Look in list. Choose the exact folder if you know it, or a disk drive, the My Computer choice, or the Network neighborhood choice as necessary.
3. If you see the desired filename, double-click it to load the presentation into PowerPoint.
4. If you don't see the file, use the Look in portion of the File Open dialog box to specify a different folder or drive.
5. If all else fails, try the Find technique described next.

FINDING "LOST" PRESENTATIONS

If you don't know where a presentation file is stored, either use the Windows 95 Find command on the Start menu (my preferred method) or use the Find features in the File Open dialog box illustrated in Figure 1.3.

1. Use the Look in list to specify the desired drive and folder location (or choose My Computer or the likely network drive).
2. Enter a partial filename in the File Name box.
3. Make sure the Files of Type box contains the option Presentations (*.ppt). Choose that option from the drop-down list if necessary.

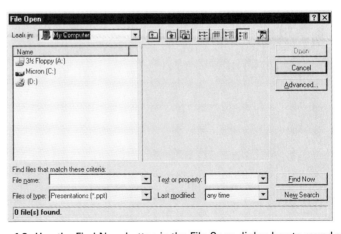

Figure 1.3 Use the Find Now button in the File Open dialog box to round up presentations.

4. Click the Advanced button.

5. When you see the Advanced Find box, click to place a checkmark in the Search subfolders box, then click the Find Now button.

6. You should soon see one or more files meeting your search criteria.

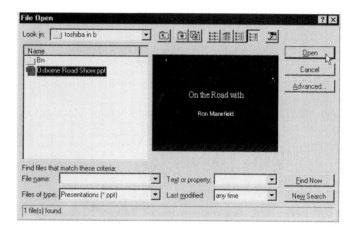

7. Double-click the desired filename in the resulting list.

To learn more about finding "lost files," check out my book *Windows 95 for Busy People* (Osborne/McGraw-Hill, 1996). You'll find a whole chapter devoted to the subject.

QUITTING POWERPOINT

Quit PowerPoint either with the Exit command on the File menu or by double-clicking the Close box on the far right side of the Power-Point title bar.

If necessary PowerPoint will prompt you to save or discard any unsaved changes.

WHAT'S NEXT?

Next stop: online help. Is it the quick path to wisdom or a frustrating adventure game?

CHAPTER

2

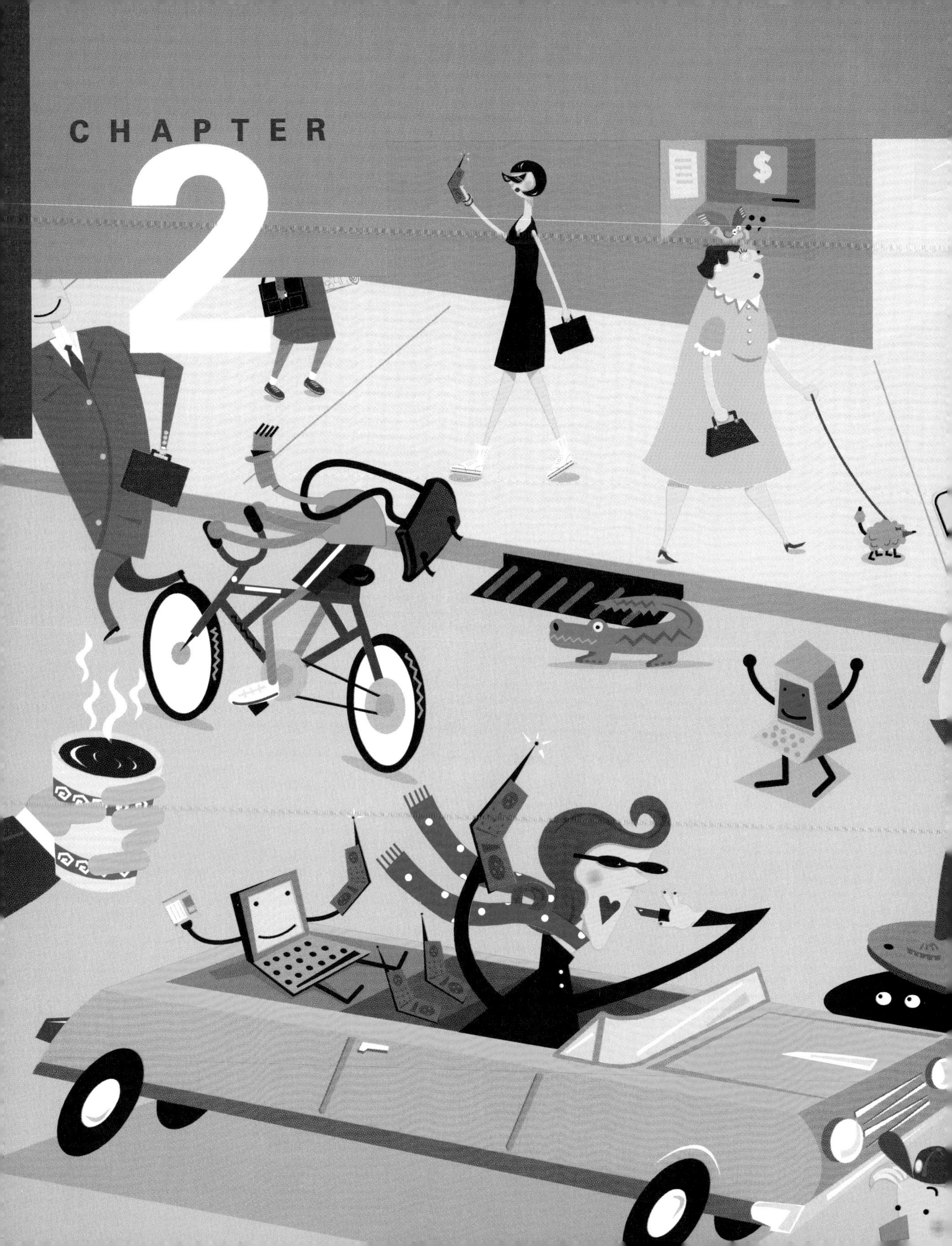

Getting Help

FAST FORWARD

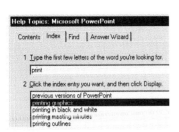

START ONLINE HELP ➤ *p. 31*

Choose Microsoft PowerPoint Help Topics from the PowerPoint
Help menu or press F1 with a PowerPoint window active.

USE HELP'S FIND TAB ➤ *pp. 32-33*

1. Choose Microsoft PowerPoint Help Topics from
   PowerPoint's Help menu or press F1. (Don't confuse
   Windows 95 Help with PowerPoint Help.)
2. Click the Find tab, if necessary, to bring it forward.
   (PowerPoint might want to index the Help files at this point.)
3. Type the word(s) of interest.
4. Double click the desired topic in resulting list.
5. ESC closes the Help window.

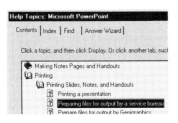

USE HELP'S INDEX TAB ➤ *pp. 34-35*

1. Choose Microsoft PowerPoint Help Topics from
   PowerPoint's Help menu or press F1.
2. Click the Index tab, if necessary, to bring it forward.
3. Type the word(s) of interest.
4. Double click the desired topic in the resulting list.
5. ESC closes the Help window.

USE HELP'S CONTENTS TAB ➤ *pp. 35-36*

1. Choose Microsoft PowerPoint Help Topics from
   PowerPoint's Help menu or press F1.
2. Click the Contents tab, if necessary, to bring it forward.
3. Double-click books to display subtopics.
4. Double-click pages to read them.
5. ESC closes the Help window.

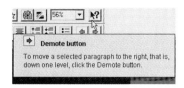

GET "WHAT'S THIS?" HELP ➤ *pp. 36-37*

1. Click the little question mark boxes in the upper-right corners of most PowerPoint windows.
2. The mouse pointer shape changes.
3. Click on buttons, sliders, and so forth.
4. Read the resulting text.
5. ESC closes the Help window.

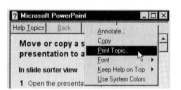

PRINTING HELP TOPICS ➤ *p. 36*

1. Make sure your printer is ready.
2. Display a Help topic.
3. Click the Options button, or right-click.
4. Choose Print Topic...
5. Set the desired options in the Print dialog box.
6. Click OK.
7. ESC closes the Help window.

GET HELP IN DIALOG BOXES ➤ *p. 37*

Many PowerPoint dialog boxes contain small Help buttons containing question marks. Clicking these buttons and pointing to objects in the dialog box frequently provides useful help.

HOVERING THE MOUSE POINTER FOR HELP ➤ *p. 30*

To see the name of many onscreen objects:

1. Position the mouse pointer over the object (a Toolbar button for instance).
2. Leave it there for a moment.
3. The item's name will often appear in a ToolTip.
4. Additional information about the item will appear on the Status bar at the bottom of the PowerPoint window.

PowerPoint provides very powerful online help features. For instance, you have just seen in the Fast Forward how hovering your mouse pointer over things often displays their names. In a moment you'll learn about a huge library of indexed Help text and how to search it. PowerPoint also provides *Answer Wizards.* Some of the help you'll receive is based upon observations PowerPoint makes about the way you work. It will even notice your bad habits and suggest better (or at least different) ones.

For tougher problems, Microsoft provides automated dial-up help. You can access it via telephone, fax, or data modem. Let's take a closer look at today's wide array of PowerPoint Help options.

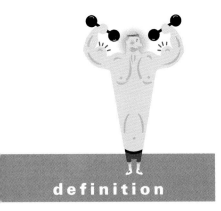

definition

Wizard: Problem-solving programs that launch, seemingly by themselves, while you are working with Windows and other Microsoft programs. Wizards ask you multiple-choice questions and then either fix problems, or change settings, or tell you something.

DON'T CONFUSE WINDOWS HELP WITH POWERPOINT HELP

Windows 95 and PowerPoint both offer Help. Sometimes it's easy to get confused. At the risk of oversimplifying this, if your question is about your computer itself (the display, memory, sound, disk drives, and so on) start your journey in the Windows 95 Help system. Windows Help is available from the Windows Start menu. PowerPoint Help is found on the Help menu located on the PowerPoint menu bar.

If you have questions specific to PowerPoint, try the PowerPoint Help feature. For more esoteric problems (like importing obscure graphic formats, advanced font trivia, and the like, try dial-up resources like the Microsoft Network, Microsoft's WWW (World Wide Web) site, America Online, CompuServe, and so forth. These external sources of information are often more current and complete than the Help files shipped with PowerPoint. And don't forget to rub elbows in the various user-to-user areas of these dial-up sites.

OPENING THE POWERPOINT HELP WINDOW

Choose Microsoft PowerPoint Help Topics from PowerPoint's Help menu or press F1. You'll see a window like the one in Figure 2.1.

With this window in front of you, you can choose to see Help organized in "books" (using the Contents tab), or view an alphabetical list of topics (via the Index tab), or type a keyword or phrase (in the Find tab) and see what happens. Then there is the Answer Wizard tab. It lets you ask "natural language" questions like "Tell me about Page Setup" and get answers or at least a list of related Help topics. My personal favorite form of Help comes from the Find tab.

Displays an alphabetized list of Help topics

Lets you search for particular terms and displays a list of corresponding topics

Click to see Help topics organized in "books"

Runs the Answer Wizard, an intelligent assistant

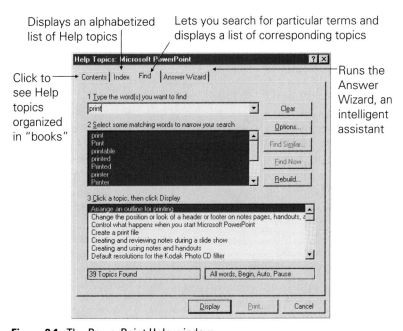

Figure 2.1 The PowerPoint Help window

SEARCHING FOR WORDS AND PHRASES IN HELP

Suppose you want to find out about sorting (rearranging) slides.

1. Choose Microsoft PowerPoint Help Topics from the PowerPoint Help menu or press F1.
2. Click the Find tab if necessary to bring it forward. (The very first time you do this, the Help software might display a Help Wizard asking you what kind of database you'd like to set up. Click the Next button and then click Finish if this happens.)
3. Type the word or phrase of interest (**sort**, for example).

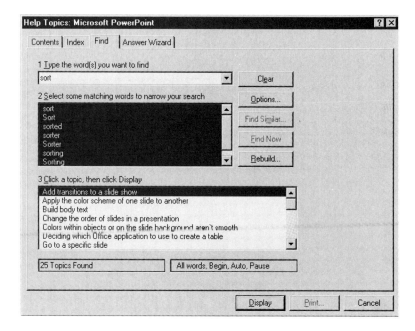

4. Either scroll through the list of topics and double-click one or type an additional word to narrow the search. Here, simply double-clicking "Change the order of the slides in a presentation" gets you the answer you need:

habits & strategies

You can frequently leave Help topics open as you try the prescribed steps. Just drag and perhaps resize the Help window so it fits in some out-of-the-way location on your screen. This eliminates the need to memorize or print.

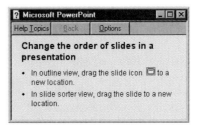

5. Use the Close box or the ESC key to quit Help and get back to work. (Clicking the Help Topics button takes you back to the Find tab.)

HELP WINDOW TRICKS

PowerPoint Help offers numerous, subtle features that you should not ignore. Here are some of my favorites.

Buttons in Help Text

Many Help windows contain buttons nestled within the Help text. These provide additional assistance. Some of these buttons run programs, open the control panel so that you can make adjustments, and so on. Others simply provide additional information. For instance, in the illustration that follows, clicking the tiny button will provide additional information about the button's function.

habits & strategies

Try clicking those tiny buttons when you see them.

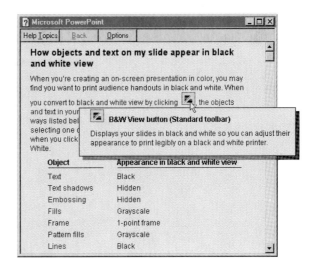

Highlighted Words Provide Definitions

Clicking the colored, underlined words in Help screens (*text attributes* in this example) provides definitions of the terms.

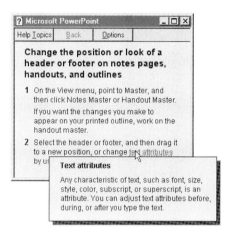

THE INDEX TAB

The Index tab in your PowerPoint Help window provides an alphabetical list of topics. You can scroll the list with the PAGE UP, PAGE DOWN and other navigational keyboard keys, or with the scroll tools and your mouse, or by typing the first few characters of a topic. For instance, typing **back** gets you in the background colors neighborhood, albeit not as gracefully as with the Find tab. Use the following steps to locate your topic of interest.

1. Choose Microsoft PowerPoint Help Topics from PowerPoint's Help menu or press F1.
2. Click the Index tab, if necessary, to bring it forward.
3. Type the first few letters of the word or phrase of interest.
4. Add more letters if this helps focus the search. (Backspace to delete if you've narrowed too much.)
5. Double-click on the desired topic in the list. (This often produces a new list of topics.)
6. Select a topic from the list, and double-click to read it.

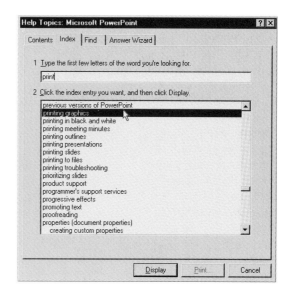

THE CONTENTS TAB

The Contents tab presents you with tiny pictures of books. These books contain books within them, and the books contain little Help pages upon which you click. I never cared for this Contents tab approach, but try it. You might like it.

1. Choose Microsoft PowerPoint Help Topics from PowerPoint's Help menu or press F1.
2. Click on the Contents tab, if necessary, to bring it forward.
3. Double-click an icon representing a book or the text next to the icon (*Creating, Opening, and Saving Presentations,* for example).
4. Double-click another book (*Finding Files,* perhaps).
5. Double-clicking pages (icons) with question marks displays the Help topic.
6. Read and perhaps print the topic.
7. To learn more, click any buttons or colored words you might find in the Help topic (such as definitions).
8. Use the Close box or the ESC key to quit Help. (Clicking the Help Topics button takes you back to the Contents tab.)

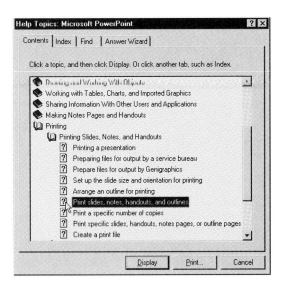

PRINTING AND COPYING HELP TOPICS

You can print Help topics once you have them on your screen. Make sure your printer is ready. Click the Options button in the Help window's button bar. Choose Print Topic. Make any necessary changes in the resulting Print dialog box (number of copies to print, and so forth). Click OK or press ENTER to start printing.

"WHAT'S THIS?" HELP

Do buttons leave you clueless? Have you always wondered what that Demote button on the Formatting toolbar does? The next time you see a gizmo that is not self-explanatory, look to the upper-right corner of the PowerPoint parent window (in the Standard toolbar) for a little button with a question mark like this one:

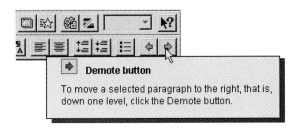

When you see the Help button:

1. Click it.
2. Your mouse pointer's appearance will change. (It gets a little tag-along question mark of its own.)
3. Point to the source of your confusion.
4. Click.
5. You will probably get an explanation.
6. Clicking a second time turns off "What's This?"

DIALOG BOX HELP

Occasionally PowerPoint will ask you a bizarre question or make some disturbing proclamation. If the dialog box causing the interruption contains a Help button (which should not be confused with the Help button in PowerPoint's Standard toolbar), give it a click. Sometimes you'll get useful assistance.

THE ANSWER WIZARD

The Answer Wizard is Microsoft's most recent attempt at commercializing artificial intelligence. The results are, well ... artificial. In theory, you simply type natural language questions (in English, for example) and the Wizard either tells you what you want to know, or shows you how to do what you want done. Sometimes the cranky old Wiz will just do what it thinks you want done. Here's an example. Suppose I want to know how to print just selected slides. I might choose Answer Wizard from the PowerPoint Help menu and type the question **"How do I print selected slides**?" The capitalization and question mark are unnecessary, since the wizard is quite forgiving about these things. In fact, you can just enter keywords like "print selected" and get the same results. Much of the Wiz's "natural language" is smoke and mirrors. It looks for keywords of interest and displays a variety of possible topics from which you pick. For example, entering either the full sentence or two keywords just mentioned causes the wizard to display the following set of Help topics.

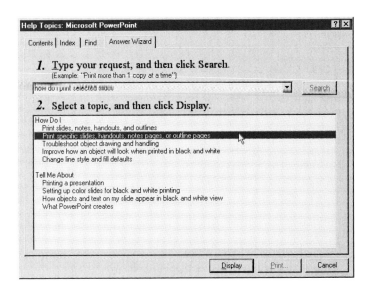

Since the closest-sounding topic is "Print slides, notes, handouts, and outlines," double-clicking it will cause the Wizard to go ahead and demonstrate the process.

The Wiz will visit the File menu for you, choose the Print command and open the dialog box, then post a little note of explanation. Clicking removes the note but leaves the dialog box where you can do what you were told to do, or press ESC to leave things alone and quit the Help exercise.

The Wizard is an amazing, entertaining, and sometimes frustrating pet. The results will vary based on how you phrase the question and how the Wizard was programmed to respond to keywords in your phrase. And, of course, human language is full of ambiguity, which confuses the heck out of computers.

USING MICROSOFT'S FAST TIPS SERVICE

Microsoft provides 24-hour, 365-day technical support via fax and prerecorded voice tips. You access these tireless slaves from any touch tone-equipped phone, fax, or modem. Since all busy people have fax machines, I assume you do too.

From any phone (it need not be your fax phone), dial 800-936-4100 for help with Windows 95, PowerPoint, and other desktop applications (Word, and so forth).

1. Listen to the choices.
2. Use your phone's touch-tone pad to request a "map" or catalog of available documents and recordings.
3. Enter your fax telephone number when prompted to do so. (Be sure the fax machine or modem is ready to receive.)
4. When you have been told that the document will be faxed, hang up and watch another tree fall on your behalf.
5. Call back with map in hand and request the desired information.

DIALING UP THE MICROSOFT NETWORK FOR HELP

If your computer is modem-equipped, and if you have set up your Microsoft Network account, you might find the help you need in Microsoft's Knowledge Base, or perhaps in the User-to-User areas. Table 2.1 provides a few resources to get you started.

Resource	Reach via	Notes
Microsoft Knowledge Base and Software Library	America Online, CompuServe, The Microsoft Network, Microsoft's WWW site (see below), and others	An amazing collection of tips, work-arounds, bug reports, files, and more.
Microsoft's World Wide Web Server	http://www.microsoft.com/	Where do you want to go today? Even job postings here!
Users Groups	The Computing sections of America Online, CompuServe, Prodigy, and others. (Many neighborhood users groups have their own BBSs too.)	Don't confuse the *experts* with the *wannabe* experts. Advice in these groups runs the gamut from brilliant to dangerous.

Table 2.1 Dial-up Help resources

OTHER SOURCES OF AUTOMATED HELP

There are perhaps a thousand or more online sources of Windows 95 and Windows application-related help. Many of these resources provide lists of other places to graze. Just remember. No overnight camping. You are busy!

To learn more about outside sources of help, type **help** in the Find tab of the PowerPoint Help dialog box and double-click the topic Connect to Microsoft technical resources. Click the various buttons to learn more.

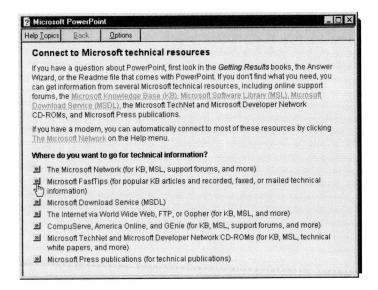

WHAT'S NEXT

In Chapter 3, you'll discover how to quickly outline an entire presentation using the AutoContent Wizard.

DO NOT DISTURB

Quick Outlining with Content Wizards

INCLUDES

- Starting the AutoContent Wizard

- Types of available content outlines

- Entering and editing text and graphics

- Editing the Wizard's work

FAST FORWARD

START THE AUTOCONTENT WIZARD ➤ p. 47

- Choose AutoContent Wizard in the PowerPoint window at startup, or
- Choose New from the File menu, then double-click the AutoContent Wizard icon in the Presentations tab of the New Presentation window, or
- If you have Microsoft Office, use the Office toolbar's Start a New Document button, click the Presentations tab, then double-click the AutoContent Wizard icon.

CREATE TITLE SLIDES ➤ p. 48

1. After starting the AutoContent Wizard and clicking Next to pass the Wizard's "welcome" screen, you will be asked to enter or edit your name, then enter or edit a title and subtitle for your presentation.
2. Enter or edit the text by clicking in the box needing changes and entering or editing text normally.
3. Click the Next button to proceed.

SELECT PRESENTATION TYPES ➤ p. 48

1. When the AutoContent Wizard asks, click to choose Recommending a Strategy, Selling a Product, Service, or Idea, or any of the four other presentation type choices.
2. If you don't see a choice you like, click the Other button and pick a presentation type from the resulting list, then click OK.
3. Click Next.

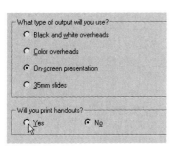

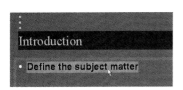

SELECT A VISUAL STYLE AND LENGTH ➤ *pp. 48-49*

1. If asked, pick Professional, Contemporary, or the Default visual style by clicking the corresponding button. (*Professional* provides a white marble look, while *Contemporary* provides a blue background with a globe logo and dark blue lines. *Default* chooses the style normally associated with the presentation type. Don't fret. You can change styles later.)

2. When asked the desired length of the presentation, choose 30 Minutes or less, More than 30 minutes, or Haven't decided. (This changes the number of entries in the automated outlines for many presentations. When in doubt, pick Haven't decided, which serves as the default.)

3. Click Next to define an output format or Finish to go directly to the new slides.

SELECT AN OUTPUT FORMAT ➤ *p. 49*

1. PowerPoint's format default will design your presentation for viewing on your computer's screen. If you prefer, you can specify Black and white overheads, Color overheads, or 35mm slides by selecting one of those choices when the Wizard asks.

2. If you plan to print handouts, click the Yes button.

3. Click the Finish button to skip the "Congratulations" screen and proceed to the slides themselves.

ADD AND EDIT TEXT ➤ *pp. 51-52*

- When working in Templates, click text placeholders (PowerPoint labels like *Click to add title*, and so on), then type to enter new text.

- To edit existing text, click to position the insertion point, or drag to select, or double-click to word select. Then edit as you would in any other Windows-savvy program.

- See Chapter 5 for more information about text.

ADD AND EDIT GRAPHICS ➤ *pp. 51-52*

- When slides contain placeholders for graphics, double-click the placeholder and follow the onscreen instructions.
- To insert graphics where there are no graphic placeholders, use the Insert command.
- See Chapter 6 for more information about graphics.

Have you ever sat in a meeting and wondered if you were experiencing déjà vu? Sadly, many, many business meetings are much the same—same topics, same organization, very similar content. Now with the AutoContent Wizard you can create a quick, punchy presentation to make any meeting more memorable.

OFF TO SEE THE WIZARD!

The AutoContent Wizard asks you several questions and then uses a predefined template containing suggested topics and tips to help you tell your story. These templates even contain content outlines for everyday meetings. There are templates for:

Breaking bad news	Training sessions
General presentations	Business plans
Progress reports	Brainstorming sessions
Sales presentations	Marketing meetings
Strategy meetings	Employee orientations

When you start PowerPoint and dismiss the tip of the day, you will be presented with the PowerPoint dialog box. It offers a number of choices. If you desire help with the content of your presentation, click the AutoContent Wizard button, then click the OK button to get started.

SHORTCUT

You can start a new Wizard-driven presentation at any time by choosing New from the File menu. (The AutoContent Wizard icon is in the Presentations tab of the New Presentation dialog box.)

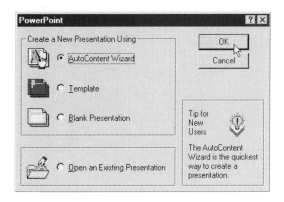

After you read the Wizard's greeting, click the Next button (or press ENTER). You'll see the second dialog box.

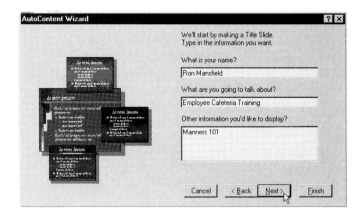

Here, you are asked to provide information for the title slide (the opening slide in your presentation). Type a topic, change the name in the name box if necessary, and place other text in the Other information you'd like to display? text area, if you wish. When you click Next, you will see a list of presentation types (Strategy, Selling, Training, and so on). A summary of each choice appears on the right side of the dialog box as you click on a presentation type.

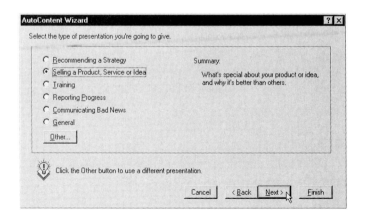

Depending on the type of presentation you select, you might see a dialog box which lets you make a few more decisions about how your presentation will look. If you don't see a topic you like, try the Other

habits & strategies

If you are using your own computer, the name in the What is your name? box should be correct. PowerPoint gets this information from the registered user's name. Change the name in the Windows Control Panel if it is wrong.

button. It will provide you with a list of additional templates, and a chance to preview their appearance.

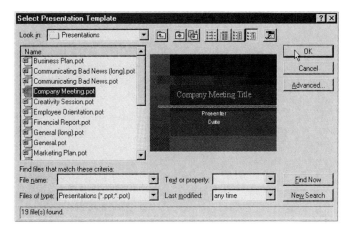

Double-click the template of your choice to return to the Wizard.

When you settle on a topic (Training, for example), click the Next button to move on. You can also tell AutoContent how long you want your presentation to run in this dialog box. Click Next when you are satisfied with the settings.

The penultimate AutoContent box is where you specify what kind of output you want. You can also tell the Wizard whether you want handouts of your presentation.

SHORTCUT

If you know what the rest of the dialog boxes do and their settings are acceptable, you can click Finish at any time to create the presentation.

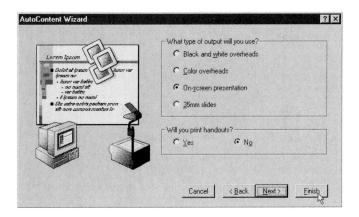

Click Finish when you're ready to move on (Next just takes you to a needless "Congratulations" dialog box). You will get the racing flag dialog box (the last box). Click the Outline View button to see an outline of the presentation. Figure 3.1 shows the beginning of a Training presentation.

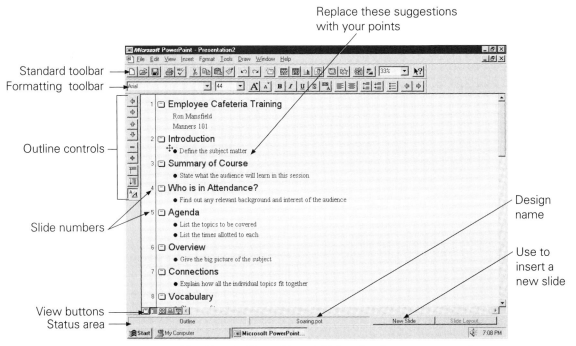

Figure 3.1 The Wizard will provide an initial outline for your presentation, complete with content suggestions.

upgrade note

The Wizard no longer automatically switches to PowerPoint's Outline view, but it's a good idea to visit the outline first. Click on the Outline View button if you aren't already in Outline view. You will see a number of slides. In Outline view, the slides are numbered along the left edge of the window.

Notice that the Wizard has already edited the title slide for you. It inserts the topic and presenter's name information that you typed earlier.

EDITING THE WIZARD'S WORK

Edit PowerPoint text just as you do Word or Excel text. As you can see in Figure 3.1, the PowerPoint window has scroll bars, toolbars, and all the other things you've come to expect. Select text to edit or replace it. Figure 3.2 shows some selected text.

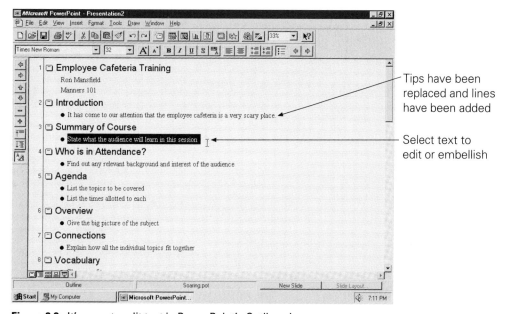

Tips have been replaced and lines have been added

Select text to edit or embellish

Figure 3.2 It's easy to edit text in PowerPoint's Outline view.

You already know the important text-editing techniques well if you've ever used another Windows program. Here's a brief review. (Details can be found in Chapter 5.)

- Select text by dragging or double-clicking.
- Type to replace selected text.
- Use toolbar buttons and drop-down lists to embellish (bold, underline, and so on).
- To insert text, point and click to move the insertion point and then start typing.
- Press ENTER to insert new bullet items.

- Use the DELETE key to remove text and bullets.
- Most other tools (like drag and drop or cut and paste) work in PowerPoint.

SAVE YOUR WORK

As a reminder, it's a good idea to save your work early and often. This way, if you make a mess of things, you can abandon your mistakes and reload the previously saved version. Saving regularly will also help you out-wit the computer reliability gods.

WHAT'S NEXT?

In Chapter 4 we'll explore Design templates—ways to change the overall look of your presentations.

CHAPTER 4

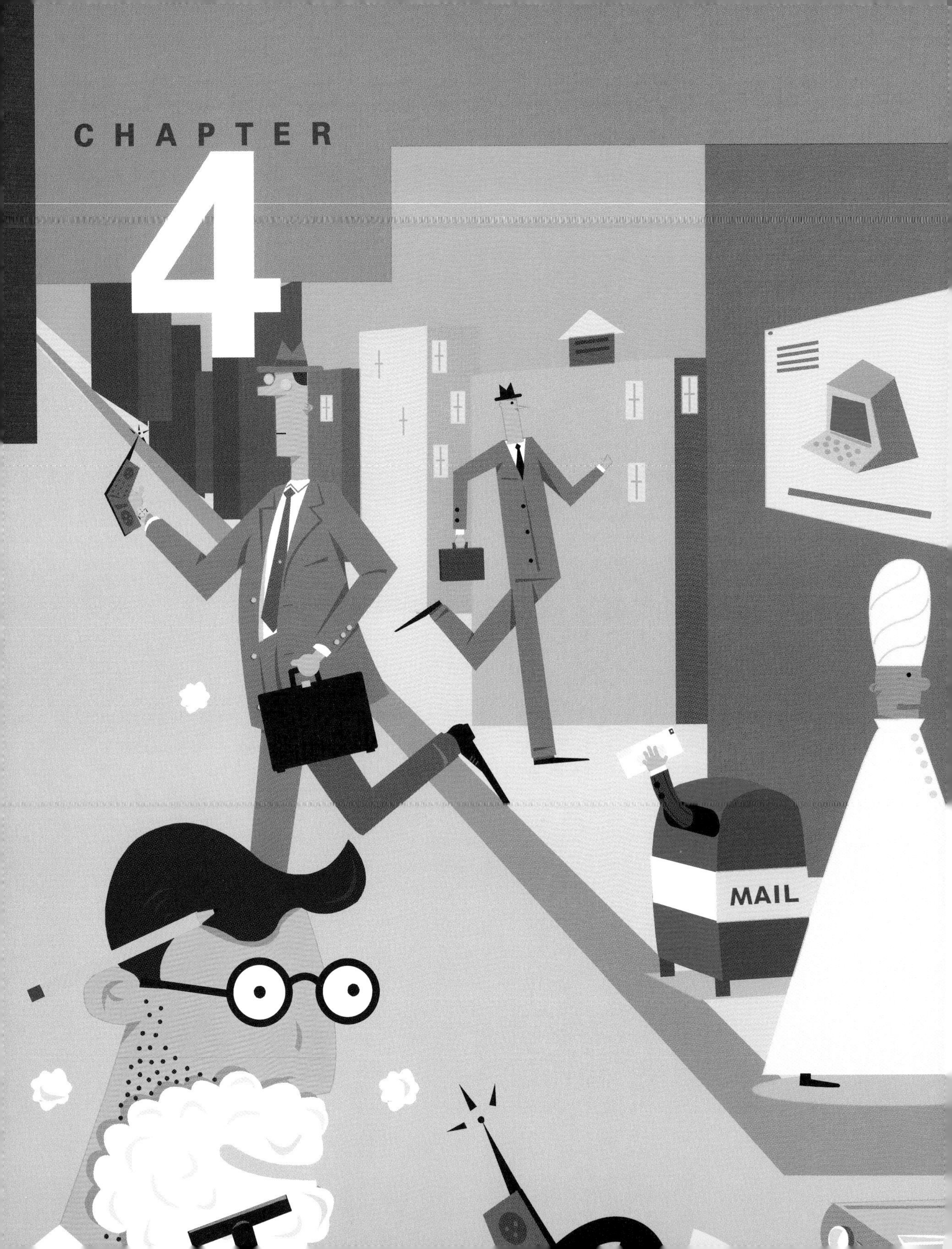

Design Templates, Color Schemes, and Masters

FAST FORWARD

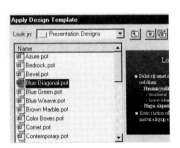

PREVIEW DESIGN TEMPLATES ➤ p. 63

1. Open an existing presentation or start a new one.
2. Choose Apply Design Template from the Format menu.
3. Click the name of a template that looks interesting.
4. Watch the preview in the Preview box.
5. Use the UP ARROW and DOWN ARROW keys to preview other templates.

EMPLOY A DESIGN TEMPLATE FOR THE ENTIRE PRESENTATION ➤ p. 63

1. Open an existing presentation or start a new one.
2. Choose Apply Design Template from the Format menu.
3. Click the name of a template that looks interesting.
4. Confirm that this is the desired template by checking the preview in the Preview box.
5. Click Apply.
6. PowerPoint will apply the template's settings to the entire presentation.

CHANGE SLIDE COLOR SCHEMES ➤ pp. 64-65

1. Open an existing presentation or start a new one.
2. If you only want to change one slide, display that slide.
3. Choose Slide Color Scheme from the Format menu.
4. Click a possible scheme in the Color Schemes dialog box.
5. Click Preview if desired.
6. Click Apply to All to change the entire presentation or Apply to affect only the currently displayed slide.
7. Check your presentation. Use Undo if the new scheme causes problems.

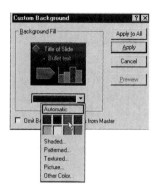

CHANGE BACKGROUND FILL COLORS ➤ *pp. 66-67*

1. Open an existing presentation or start a new one.
2. If you only want to change one slide, display that slide.
3. Choose Custom Background from the Format menu.
4. Click the drop-down menu and pick a background color.
5. Click Preview if desired.
6. Click Apply to All to change the entire presentation or Apply to affect only the currently displayed slide.
7. Check your presentation. Use Undo if the new background color causes problems.

SUPPRESS BACKGROUND GRAPHICS ➤ *pp. 67-68*

1. Open an existing presentation or start a new one.
2. If you only want to change one slide, display that slide.
3. Choose Custom Background from the Format menu.
4. Click to place a checkmark in the Omit Background Graphics from Master box.
5. Click Preview if desired.
6. Click Apply to All to change the entire presentation or Apply to affect only the currently displayed slide.
7. Use Undo to restore the graphic or repeat steps 1-6, removing the checkmark in step 4.

CREATE CUSTOM DESIGN TEMPLATES ➤ *p. 70*

1. Start a new presentation (using an existing template with content, if you like).
2. Change the color scheme, master contents, and so on.
3. Add any text, slides, graphics, or other elements you want to establish as standard elements in new projects.
4. Check your work (spelling, capitalization consistency, and so on).
5. Choose Save As in the menu.
6. Pick a type from the drop-down list to save the presentation as a presentation template in the Presentations folder usually located in the MSOffice folder (C:\MSOffice\Templates\ Presentations). To see the template listed under the General tab, store it in the MSOffice Templates folder (C:\MSOffice\Templates).

USE SOMEONE ELSE'S TEMPLATES ➤ *p. 70*

- Copy other people's templates (files ending with the extension .pot) into your templates folder—typically C:\MSOffice\Templates\Presentations.
- Alternately you can use the PowerPoint Open command or the Windows 95 Find feature to load templates residing on networked drives or on disks other than your primary hard drive, or in folders other than your Templates folder.

CHANGE THE DEFAULT TEMPLATE FOR NEW PRESENTATIONS ➤ *p. 71*

1. Start a new presentation (using an existing template with content, if you like).
2. Change the color scheme, master contents, and so on.
3. Add any text, slides, graphics, or other elements you want to establish as standard elements in most new projects.
4. Check your work (spelling, capitalization consistency, and so on).
5. Choose Save As in the File menu.
6. Pick Presentation Templates (*.pot) from the drop-down Save as type list.
7. Save the presentation using the filename Blank Presentation.pot in the Templates folder (usually located in the MSOffice folder).
8. Answer Yes when asked if you wish to replace the old default format.

Alternately, you can delete the template Blank Presentation.pot and copy or rename a different Microsoft-provided template. Its name must be Blank Presentation.pot and it must reside in the Templates folder, usually found in the MSOffice folder.

One of the key differences between PowerPoint and a word processing program like Microsoft Word is that PowerPoint makes it easy to combine background colors, colored text, and other design elements. In this chapter you will learn about *design templates, color schemes,* and *masters*—all shortcuts to great-looking presentatins.

THE ROLE OF DESIGN TEMPLATES, COLOR SCHEMES, AND MASTERS

Remember when you used the AutoContent Wizard in Chapter 3, and it asked questions about topics, visual style, presentation length, type of output, and so on? The Wizard was helping you choose from among a variety of standard templates, color schemes, and masters. Frequently the Wiz will give you just what you need. But if you have the urge to create unique, custom-looking presentations, you might want to take more control over the design choices and options.

While you *can* manually pick and choose virtually every design element, the process can be time consuming and tedious. Besides, you are too busy to be distracted by such details as which background colors look best with which text colors. Fortunately, there's a middle ground. Masters, color schemes, and design templates let you specify all of these appearance elements easily. Let's look at how they all work together.

Masters

As you might remember from the brief introduction in Chapter 1, and as you saw in Chapter 2, Masters are slides where you define (or someone else defines) the overall formatting to be used in a presentation. Each presentation has four masters. There's a master for your presentation's slides, another master for your presentation's titles, another for handouts, and another for your speaker's notes. Figure 4.1

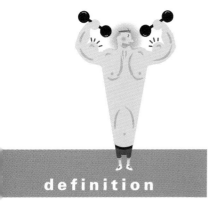

definition

AutoContent Wizard:

A computerized assistant that asks you questions about your presentation needs and gets you started in a hurry. See Chapter 3 for details.

Figure 4.1 A typical slide master.

shows a typical slide master. The masters define things like the typestyle and size used on each slide or handout in a presentation.

Slide masters also have things called *master styles*. These are predefined slide layouts that make it easy to drop in text, graphics, and organizational charts. Other styles facilitate creating bulleted lists, and so on. Here are miniature representations of some typical master styles:

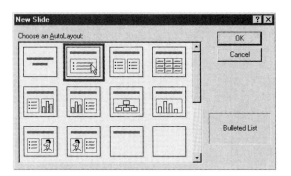

Color Schemes

In addition to masters, there are color schemes. Think of these as definitions of color combinations. Elements of a color scheme include the background color, text colors, fill colors, accent colors, and so on. PowerPoint provides a variety of predefined color schemes, and you can define others of your own.

Design Templates

When you choose a design template, its settings are applied to your entire presentation. As you will see later in this chapter, you can override settings on individual slides if you like.

A design template is a collection of all of the masters for a presentation along with its color scheme and perhaps some "boiler-plate" text that you wish to use each time you create a presentation of a certain kind. For example, you might create a template that you use for monthly progress report meetings containing text detailing your standard agenda.

USING MICROSOFT'S DESIGN TEMPLATES

You can create your own templates as you will see later in this chapter, or you can use some predefined templates provided by Microsoft. You can use these canned templates either as-is, or as a starting point for your own creations. Simply changing the design template used with a presentation can really alter its appearance. For example, Figure 4.2 illustrates a presentation using the Blue Diagonal design template and Figure 4.3 is the same slide formatted using the Wet Sand template. Whoa!

Moreover, you can pick a design template when you start a project, or start out with PowerPoint's "Standard Presentation" template to enter and arrange your presentation, then apply different templates until you get a pleasing "look."

habits & strategies

It is usually better to pick a design template when you start a project since sometimes text and graphics that look great in one design are cramped or unattractive in another.

Previewing Design Templates

You can get a rough idea of how a template will look by previewing it in the Presentations tab of the New Presentations dialog box (although you will get a better understanding of the final look by seeing full-screen

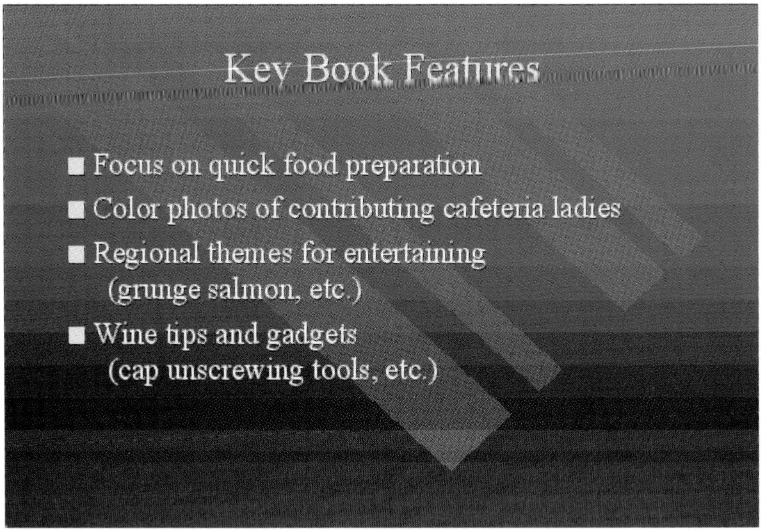

Figure 4.2 A slide formatted with the Blue Diagonal Design template.

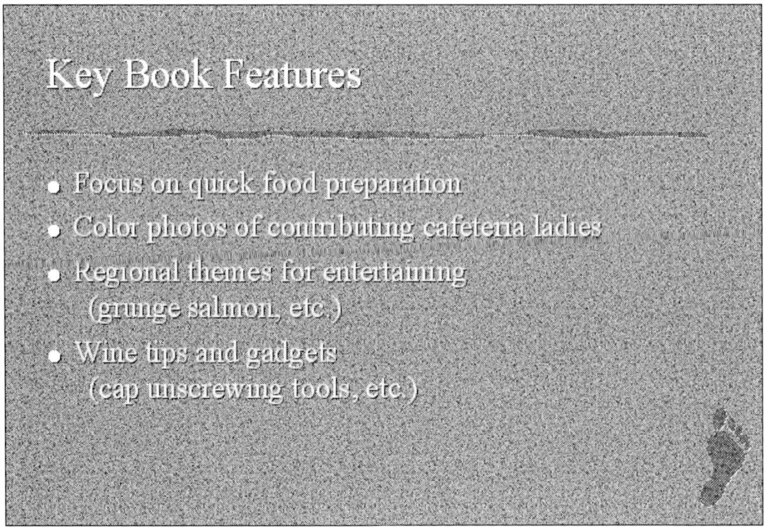

Figure 4.3 The same slide shown in Figure 4.2, but this time formatted with the Wet Sand design template.

versions). First, let's see how to take a quick peek at the miniatures, then we'll explore the full-screen method.

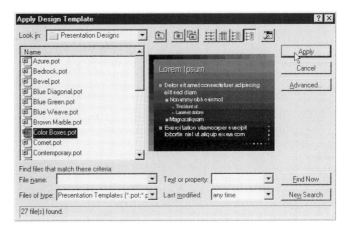

1. Open an existing presentation or start a new one.
2. Choose Apply Design Template from the Format menu.
3. Click the name of a template that looks interesting.
4. Watch the preview in the preview box.
5. Use the UP ARROW and DOWN ARROW keys to preview other templates.

Previewing Design Templates in Their Full Size

To see a larger version of the design while in Slide view, follow the preceding steps and either click the Apply button or double-click the desired design. If you are creating a new presentation, PowerPoint will open a new template where you can add the desired text.

Applying the Chosen Design to a Presentation

Once you have selected a design, click the Apply button in the Apply Design Template dialog box. Examine each of your slides to see if you like the overall look of the presentation. If you don't, you can use the Undo command on the Edit menu, or simply repeat the previously described steps and pick a different design.

SHORTCUT

To switch to Slide View mode, use the view buttons in the lower-left corner of your screen.

CHANGING SLIDE COLOR SCHEMES

Design Templates provide suggested color schemes that are configured to look best under specific circumstances. For example, some color schemes enhance 35mm slide readability, other schemes look better on your computer screen, and so on. You can choose from the schemes provided with the templates, or make your own (if you have the time and the inclination, busy person that you are). To preview and select standard, available color scheme choices for a design template:

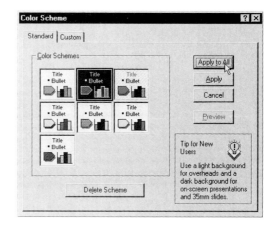

1. Open an existing presentation or start a new one. Make sure you are using the desired design template.
2. If you only want to change one slide, display that slide.
3. Choose Slide Color Scheme from the Format menu.
4. Click a possible scheme in the Color Scheme dialog box.
5. Click Preview if desired.
6. Click Apply to All to change the entire presentation or Apply to affect only the currently displayed slide.
7. Check your presentation. Use Undo if the new scheme causes problems.

A color scheme can make a big difference in the overall look of your presentation. For example, Figures 4.4 and 4.5 show the same slide formatted with the same design template, but with two different color schemes.

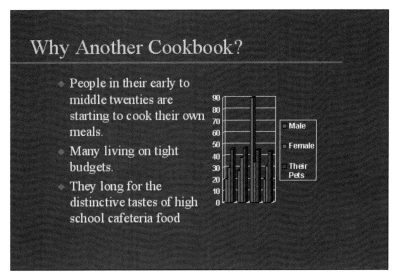

Figure 4.4 A slide with the design template's default color scheme.

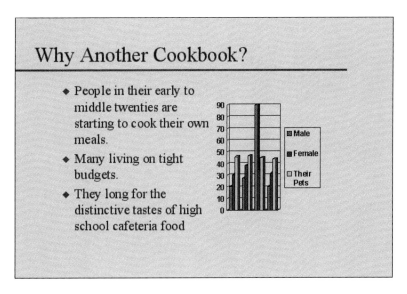

Figure 4.5 The same slide as shown in Figure 4.4, but with a different color scheme employed.

CHANGING BACKGROUNDS

Okay, gadget junkies background fiddling can seriously distract you from real work. (It's *so much fun* that I played for several hours and I'll probably be late submitting this chapter because of it.) So, how could I refrain from telling you about something this entertaining?

All design templates come with colored backgrounds. They also frequently include graphics, lines, and other design elements. For example, Figure 4.6 uses the Bedrock design template with a blue background and that stone-looking graphic element.

Figure 4.6 The standard bedrock template with its blue background and rock-like-graphic.

Changing Background Colors

To change the background color, follow these simple steps:

1. Open an existing presentation or start a new one.
2. If you only want to change one slide, display that slide.
3. Choose Custom Background from the Format menu.

4. Click the drop-down menu and click a color sample from the pallet to pick a background color.
5. Click Preview if desired.
6. Click Apply to All to change the entire presentation or Apply to affect only the currently displayed slide.
7. Check your presentation. Use Undo if the new background color causes problems.

For example, Figure 4.7 shows the same slide as the one in Figure 4.6, but with a maroonish background. Notice the blue line at the rock's edge. That's because the rock graphic includes a blue shadow. Experiment!

Figure 4.7 The Bedrock template with a background color change.

Suppressing Background Graphics

What if you like the look of a design but hate the background graphic? Or what if the graphic gets in the way of your own words or graphics? For example, in the next illustration the globe and the graph seem to be fighting each other for attention.

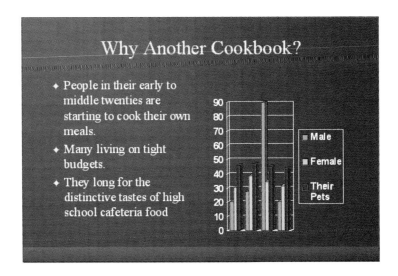

Follow these steps to eliminate the graphic elements provided by a design template:

1. Open an existing presentation or start a new one.
2. If you only want to change one slide, display that slide.
3. Choose Custom Background from the Format menu.
4. Click to place a checkmark in the Omit Background Graphics from Master box.
5. Click Preview if desired.
6. Click Apply to All to change the entire presentation or Apply to affect only the currently displayed slide.
7. Use Undo to restore the graphic or repeat steps 1-6, removing the checkmark in step 4.

You'll learn more about graphics in Chapter 6.

Dropping in Your Own Background Graphics

Well, if you are a budding Georgia O'Keeffe or Helmut Newton, and if you are interested in using your own or someone else's graphics as backgrounds—photos, drawings, or whatnot—you can accomplish this easily. For example, Figure 4.8 shows that Bedrock-formatted template title slide with a stock photo in place of the rock graphic. Nice, huh?

And yes, you can combine the graphics provided with the template and your own. This is illustrated in Figure 4.9. Voilà!

Figure 4.8 A title slide formatted with the Bedrock design template with a photo used as the replacement background.

Figure 4.9 The Bedrock template format with the graphic intact and a photo added.

CREATING YOUR OWN DESIGN TEMPLATES

The process of creating and saving your own design templates is quite straightforward. You can start with an existing presentation or use a Microsoft-provided design template as the jumping-off point:

1. Start a new presentation (using an existing template with content, if you like).
2. Change the color scheme, master contents, and so on.
3. Add any text, slides, graphics, or other elements you want to establish as standard elements in new projects.
4. Check your work (spelling, capitalization consistency, and so on).
5. Choose Save As in the File menu.
6. Use the drop-down menu to save the presentation as a template in the Presentations folder (typically C:\MSOffice\Templates\Presentations) if you wish to see the template listed in the Presentations tab of the New dialog box. To see the template listed in the General tab, store it in the MSOffice Templates folder (C:\MSOffice\Templates).

USING OTHER PEOPLE'S TEMPLATES

You can easily copy other people's templates (files ending with the extension .pot) into your Presentations folder. It is usually located in the Templates folder, which is usually located in your MSOffice folder if you have Microsoft Office installed (C:\MSOffice\Templates\Presentations, perhaps). Once the template is there, it will show up in the Presentations tab of the New dialog box. You will also see it when you use the Office Toolbar's Start a New Document button. Again, look in the Presentations tab.

Alternately, you can use PowerPoint's Open command or the Windows 95 Find feature to load templates residing on networked drives or on disks other than your primary hard drive, or in folders other than your Templates folder.

CHANGE THE DEFAULT TEMPLATE USED IN NEW PRESENTATIONS

To have PowerPoint always begin new projects with a design of your own creation, follow these simple steps:

1. Start a new presentation (using an existing template with content, if you like).
2. Change the color scheme, master contents, and so on.
3. Add any text, slides, graphics, or other elements you want to establish as standard elements in new projects.
4. Check your work (spelling, capitalization consistency, and so on).
5. Choose Save As in the File menu.
6. Save the presentation using the filename Blank Presentation.pot in the Templates folder (usually located in the MSOffice folder).
7. Answer Yes when asked if you wish to replace the old default format.

Alternately, you can delete the template Blank Presentation.pot and copy or rename a different Microsoft-provided template. Its name must be Blank Presentation.pot and it must reside in the Templates folder, usually found in the MSOffice folder.

Since PowerPoint's text editing, graphics, and multimedia tools behave like most other Windows 95-savvy programs, you might already know how to use them.

WHAT'S NEXT?

If you are a text editing, graphics, and multimedia superstar, you might just need to skim Chapters 5 through 7, in which these topics are covered in sufficient depth to make you an effective and productive presenter. Or you could read these three chapters carefully before moving on to the subjects of rearranging, presenting, and printing.

Working with Text

FAST FORWARD

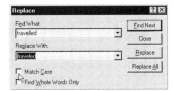

TYPE TEXT ➤ *pp. 77, 81*

1. Open a new design template or display an existing slide or note.
2. Click in text objects in slides, or position the insertion point in the desired position of your outline and type as usual. Press ENTER to finish lines, or SHIFT-ENTER if you wish to start new lines in bulleted lists without adding the next bullet.
3. Use the DELETE or BACKSPACE key to correct errors if you spot them immediately.
4. Click or tab to move from one text object to the next.
5. Be aware that excess text will not spill onto the next slide!

EDIT TEXT ➤ *pp. 80-82*

1. Drag or double-click to select text.
2. Typing over selected text or pasting will replace the selected text.
3. To insert text, click to position the insertion point, then type or paste. Text to the right and below will be pushed right and down. Remember that excess text will not spill onto the next slide!
4. Selecting and cutting text (CTRL-X) or pressing DELETE removes text. Cutting moves the text to the Clipboard, replacing the Clipboard's prior contents. Deleting does not.

FIND AND REPLACE ➤ *pp. 84-86*

1. Choose Replace from the Edit menu. (Or use the CTRL-H shortcut.)
2. Type the text you wish to replace in the Find What box (or choose it from the drop-down list).
3. Type the replacement text in the Replace With box (or choose it from the drop-down list).
4. Check Match Case if you only want to replace when the found text matches the specified capitalization.
5. Choose Find Whole Words Only to prevent replacements of text within longer text strings (like ron in elect*ron*ics).

6. Click Find to find the first occurrence, click Replace to replace, or click Find Next to skip the current occurrence and move to the next. Clicking Replace All will find and replace all occurrences without asking for repeated confirmations.

WORK IN OUTLINE VIEW ➤ *pp. 82-84*

1. Choose Outline from the View menu or click the Outline View button at the bottom of the PowerPoint window.
2. Click to select text.
3. Drag titles to rearrange slides or drag lines within slides to move them.
4. Use the Promote and Demote buttons to move lines up or down in the hierarchy.

FORMAT TEXT ➤ *pp. 90-98*

1. Select the text to be formatted.
2. Use the formatting buttons on the formatting toolbar (Bold, Italic, Shadow, and so forth) or their equivalent commands in the Font dialog box reached with the Format menu.

ASSURE CONSISTENT CASE, SPELLING, AND PUNCTUATION ➤ *pp. 98-102*

1. Finish entering your text.
2. Choose Style Checker from the Tools menu.
3. Specify the desired checks (Spelling, Visual Clarity, or Case and End Punctuation).
4. Click the Options button to change the rules used for checking. Click OK.
5. Click Start.
6. Accept or reject suggested changes.

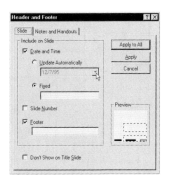

EDIT HEADER AND FOOTER TEXT, DATE STAMPS, AND NUMBERS ➤ *pp. 102-105*

1. Switch to Slide view.
2. Choose Header and Footer from the View menu.
3. Click the desired tab (Slide or Notes and Handouts).
4. Choose desired options and enter text to appear on slides and/or handouts.
5. Click Apply to change a single slide, or Apply to All to alter all slides.

Since text is one of the main ingredients in a PowerPoint presentation, and since there are so many things that you can do to alter the appearance of your words, this will be a fairly long chapter. Fortunately, if you've worked with other Windows programs, most of your existing skills are transferable. But since PowerPoint adds its own twists to text entry, editing, and formatting, be sure to at least *skim* the pages that follow.

STARTING NEW SLIDES CONTAINING TEXT

Whether you pick a design template or start your new presentation with the Blank Presentation template, you will be presented with a variety of slide layout options thanks to a PowerPoint feature called *AutoLayout.* You can choose a different slide layout for each new slide if you wish. Most of the layout choices contain areas or *text blocks* that are designed to help you enter and format text. The two most commonly-used types of text blocks are called *Title Objects* and *Body Objects*.

To choose a layout style, simply double-click the miniature representation of the desired Slide Layout from the New Slide or Slide Layout dialog box. Text blocks are represented by small lines in each miniature layout.

habits & strategies

When you click on a design in the Slide Layout dialog box, the layout's purpose is described in the small box beneath the Cancel button. Keeping an eye on this changing information will help you pick the best layout for your immediate needs.

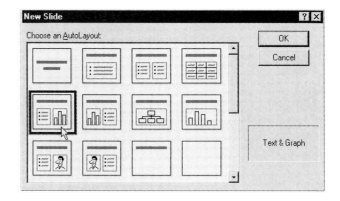

For example, in the preceding illustration, in the top row the left-most slide layout is for creating title slides with large centered text. The next layout to the right is for slides containing a title and a bulleted list. The next is for a title and two columns of bulleted lists, and so on.

The final appearance of the text is dependent upon the layout definition and overriding changes you make to the text using techniques outlined in this chapter.

TYPING TEXT

To begin typing text in Slide view, simply display the slide layout where you want to work, click in a Title Object or a Body Object, and then begin typing.

If you make a mistake and spot it immediately you can use the DELETE key to back up and correct it immediately. It is also possible to make corrections later, as you will soon see.

Keep your writing brief and to the point. Insert additional slides if necessary. While you *can* decrease type sizes and line spacing to make things fit, you shouldn't make text too much smaller or tighter than the AutoFormat defaults, or it will be difficult for audiences to read your slide, however it's displayed.

Margins Around Text

PowerPoint slides don't contain margins in the way that, say, a Microsoft Word page does. But many people think of the space around the edges of slides as margins, so that's the term I've used here. When you click to select a text object you will see an outline that defines the text object's size and shape, thereby specifying the unused space (and

thus the margins) around the object. To change the size of a text object, simply click the edge of the object and drag it to the desired size

Remember that if you position text too close to the outer edges of slides you might have trouble displaying (projecting) the text in some formats (particularly 35mm slides or overheads if you use frames).

AUTO CORRECT

The AutoCorrect feature notices when you make everyday typographical errors, then automatically corrects them. For example, if you reverse the *h* and *e* when you type the word *the* (a very common typo), PowerPoint will rearrange the incorrect text automatically.

AutoCorrect also replaces "typewriter-style" notations like (c) with special symbols like ©, the Copyright symbol.

AutoCorrect comes with a built-in list of commonly used corrections. You can edit this list and even add your own corrections. For example, you can tell AutoCorrect that you want it to replace every occurrence of pp with PowerPoint. You can also use AutoCorrect to repair common capitalization problems (although, as you will soon see, there are other features described in this chapter that might be better for fixing capitalization).

Reversing the Occasional AutoCorrection

If you are typing along and AutoCorrect "fixes" something that does not need fixing, use the Undo command on the Edit menu, the keyboard shortcut, or the Undo button on PowerPoint's Standard toolbar.

Adding Entries to the AutoCorrect List

To add an entry to the list of automatic corrections:

1. Choose AutoCorrect from the Tools menu. You will see the AutoCorrect dialog box.

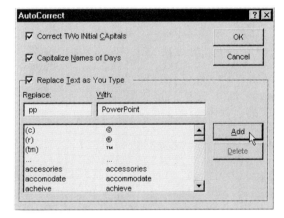

2. Type the characters you wish to replace in the Replace box (**pp**, for example).
3. Tab to the With box and enter the desired replacement (**PowerPoint**, for instance).
4. Click Add.
5. Click OK when you have finished creating new AutoCorrect entries.

**habits &
strategies**

*For major text revisions it is
often better to do your editing
in Outline view, rather than in
Slide view, using techniques
described later in this chapter.*

definition

Clipboard: *A temporary storage
area (in RAM) that can hold the
last thing you copied or cut (text,
a graphic, and so forth).*

Deleting AutoCorrect Entries

To delete an entry to the list of automatic corrections:

1. Pick AutoCorrect from the Tools menu. You will see the AutoCorrect dialog box.
2. Scroll if necessary to display the entry you wish to delete.
3. Click the entry to select it.
4. Click the Delete button.
5. Repeat steps 2-4 until done. Click OK when you have finished deleting unwanted AutoCorrect entries.

Disabling AutoCorrect

To turn off automatic corrections:

1. Pick AutoCorrect from the Tools menu. You will see the AutoCorrect dialog box.
2. Click to remove the check from the Replace Text as You Type box.
3. Click OK.

REPLACING TEXT

You can replace text by selecting words or characters, and typing to replace the selected characters. To remove text simply select it and press the DELETE key. Neither of these actions affects the contents of your Clipboard.

MOVING TEXT BY CUTTING AND PASTING

The technique you use to move text might change depending upon how much you need to move, and how far you wish to move it. When reorganizing multiple items, it is often best to work in Outline view (using techniques described in a moment). But for minor alterations, like moving a little text from one point in a title or body object to another place within the same object, you can work in Slide view. To move text from one location to another on a slide:

1. Select the text (drag to select characters or double-click to select words or click the bullet to select the whole bulleted entry).
2. Cut the selected text with the Cut command in the Edit menu, or use the CTRL-X keyboard shortcut, or the Cut button on the Standard toolbar.
3. Click to position the insertion point at the desired new location for the text.
4. Paste either by using the Paste command in the Edit menu, or the CTRL-V keyboard shortcut, or the Paste button on the Standard toolbar.

Moving Text with Drag and Drop

PowerPoint fully supports the Windows 95 Drag and Drop capability so you can also move text (and other objects) by first selecting an object, then dragging it with your mouse (notice how the shape of the mouse pointer changes). Release the mouse button to "drop" the text object.

Inserting Text

Click within a title object or body object to move the insertion point to the place in the text where you want to insert text. Begin typing (or paste the text from the Clipboard if that's where the text you are inserting resides). Text to the right of the insertion point will be pushed forward and down. Remember, text that won't fit on the current slide will *not* move to the next slide! It will just spill over the bottom of the slide in Slide view and disappear off the bottom of the screen in a slide show.

Deleting Text

Select the unwanted text and press DELETE. Text below will snake up to take its place. To delete bullets, select them and delete them like other text. Alternately you can use the Edit menu's Cut command (CTRL-X) or the scissors-like Cut button on the Formatting toolbar.

Undo and Redo

If you make a mistake while editing or reformatting text, try the Undo command which is available on the Edit menu. There is a keyboard shortcut (CTRL-Z) and an Undo button on the Standard toolbar (it looks like a counterclockwise pointing arrow). The Redo command and toolbar button can be used to "undo undos."

WORKING IN OUTLINE VIEW

Outline view is *the place* to make major renovations to the content and organization of your text. It will remind Microsoft Word wonks of *that* program's Outline view, but there are differences. Figure 5.1 shows a typical presentation in Outline view.

Promotes or demotes level of selected items
Moves items up or down
Displays more or fewer details
Shows titles only
Shows all
Shows/hides text formatting

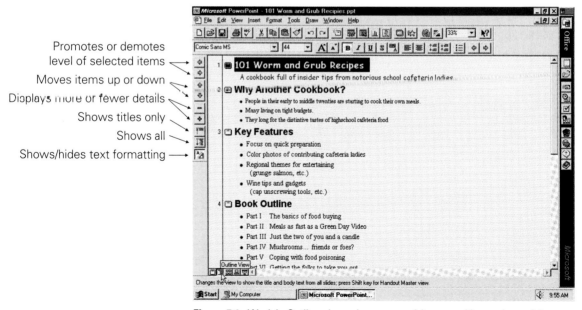

Figure 5.1 Work in Outline view when reorganizing or making major revisions.

Outline view lets you see all text or just selected heading levels. You can rearrange the order of slides by dragging them from place to place. You can move text around on its slide or move text from one slide to another. Let's take a closer look.

Expanding and Collapsing Outline Views

You can increase and decrease the amount of information displayed by clicking the buttons on the left edge of the Outline view screen. For example, to hide all the text and show just slide titles, you'd click the Show Titles button.

To reveal all the text, click the Show All button (just beneath the Show Titles button). This will bring all the text back into view.

To expand or collapse details for selected slides only (or even portions of slides):

1. Select the slide or slides, or portions thereof (SHIFT-click to select multiple slides or lines).
2. To collapse (hide detail), use the Collapse Selection button (the minus sign).
3. To expand (reveal) information in the selected area, use the Expand Selection button (the plus sign):

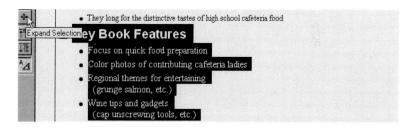

4. PowerPoint will expand the selected area so that you can see additional detail.

Promoting and Demoting Headings

Like Microsoft Word headings, PowerPoint titles and headings can have different levels. These let you quickly create multilevel indented lists like this:

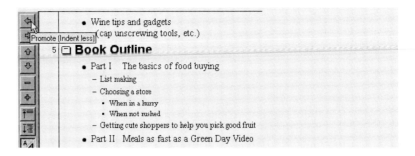

The top level is the slide title itself. The next level is for the usual bullet lists, and the next indent (*List making* and *Choosing a store* in this example) is the next level down. *When in a hurry* is yet another level further down. As you saw in Figure 5.1, different levels have their own appearance (different type size, fonts, and so forth).

To move items from one level to another, follow these steps:

1. Select an item to promote or demote.
2. Point to the bullet or icon at the left edge of the item. The mouse pointer will change to a four-headed arrow.
3. Drag left to promote or right to demote the selected item. A vertical line will appear to show you the pending new level of the item being dragged.
4. Release the mouse button. The item will take on its new indent level and appearance.

You could also just select the item and click to promote or demote In the Outlining Toolbar on the left side of the screen.

Showing and Hiding Text Formatting

Sometimes it's desirable to see Outline views without text formatting. You can get more information on the screen this way, and it may speed scrolling. Use the Show Formatting button to toggle on-screen text formatting. It's the bottom button in the Outlining toolbar collection.

FINDING AND REPLACING TEXT

PowerPoint lets you do basic text searching and replacement, though not to the degree that fancier programs like Microsoft Word permit. (Wildcards are not supported, for instance.) The Edit|Find com-

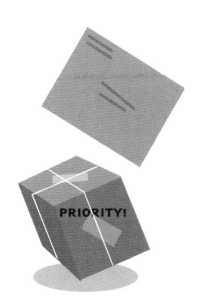

**habits &
strategies**

PowerPoint does not have a "Go To" feature like Microsoft Word's or Excel's. Find can be of some help here, though: Enter things like slide titles or unique text that you know is on a particular slide, and you can scoot from place to place that way.

mand lets you search for text and the Edit|Replace command lets you search for and change text. The usual cautions apply here. Automatic replacements can make guacamole out of a great presentation, so save your work before replacing, then check to see how it went.

Finding

Finding is actually a subset of replacing—the Find dialog box in PowerPoint includes a Replace button if you decide to expand your Find operation into a Replace operation.

1. Choose Find from the Edit menu.
2. Specify the text you are looking for in the Find What box.
3. Specify any restrictions (Match Case or Find Whole Words Only).

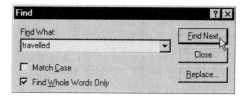

4. Use the Find Next button to find matches or Close to quit.

If you wish to replace a word after finding this way, click the Replace button. You'll be visited by the Replace dialog box, discussed in the preceding section.

Replacing

Replacing is pretty self-explanatory. For instance, to replace all occurrences of *travelled* with *traveled* you would:

1. Save your presentation.
2. Choose Replace from the Edit menu.
3. Enter **travelled** in the Find What box.
4. Enter **traveled** in the Replace With box.

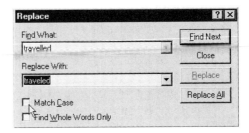

5. If you want to find only words with matching capitalization, choose Match Case.
6. To find only exact word matches (*Ron* but not elect*ronic*, for instance) choose Find Whole Words Only.
7. Click Find Next. PowerPoint will search for a match.
8. Click Replace to replace the first match, and Find Next to continue, or Replace All to replace all occurrences.
9. Check your work.

CREATING LISTS

The easy way to create bulleted lists is to pick slide layouts designed with list making in mind. They usually have the words Bulleted List in their description. Remember. You can tell a layout's function by reading the layout's description in the Slide Layout dialog box.

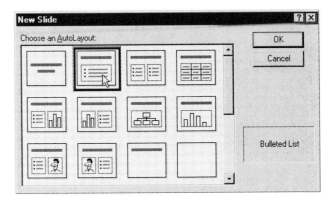

Every time you type a line for a bulleted list and press ENTER, PowerPoint will create a new bulleted line. To type on a new line without adding a bullet, hold down SHIFT when you press ENTER.

Rearranging Lines in Lists

When you position the mouse pointer over a bullet in a list, the pointer changes shape (it becomes a four-headed arrow). Drag items to their new position in the list and release the mouse button.

Deleting Lines from Lists

To delete a line in a bulleted list, select it and press DELETE. Lines below will move up to fill the gap. Undo works here if you delete the wrong line accidentally.

Inserting Lines in Lists

To insert an additional line, position the insertion point (click) at the end of the line before where you want the new line to appear. For example, if you want to insert a new line between the old lines 1 and 2, place the insertion point at the end of line 1. Then press ENTER to insert the line. Either type or paste the new text after adding the line.

Picking Bullet Styles for Lists

You can use virtually any character from any font as a bullet in the bullet lists. You have control over the size and color of bullets as well.

1. Select the bulleted items you wish to modify.
2. Choose Bullet from the Format menu to open the Bullet dialog box.
3. Choose a font to explore in the Bullets From list.
4. To get an enlarged view of your candidates while still in the dialog box, click on individual symbols.

5. Specify a different color if you wish (not possible in Outline view).
6. Click the Preview button to see the proposed changes at work.
7. The size of the bullets is specified as a percentage of the text size. Use the Size text box to change this percentage if you wish.
8. Click OK to make the change or Cancel to abort.

My technical editor reminds me that the table feature requires you to have Microsoft Word installed since the tables actually come from Word's table feature.

CREATING TABLES

The easy way to create tables (rows and columns of words and numbers) is to pick slide layouts designed for table creation. They usually have the word *table* in their description. Don't forget. You can tell a layout's function by reading the layout's description in the Slide Layout dialog box. Follow these steps:

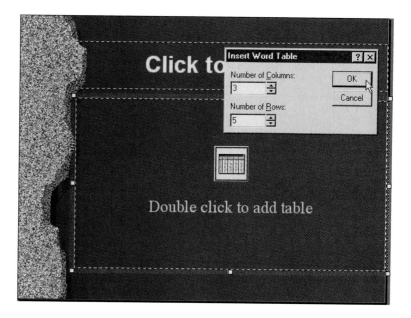

1. Switch to Slide view, if necessary.
2. Click the New Slide button to display the New Slide dialog box.
3. Select a layout designed for table making.
4. Double-click the table icon on the new slide.
5. Specify the number of columns and rows in the dialog box that appears.
6. PowerPoint will make a table of the desired dimensions (configuration).
7. Type text in the tables, tabbing or clicking to get to the desired table cell.

Adding and Deleting Rows or Columns in Tables

Use the appropriate commands on the PowerPoint Table menu to add or delete columns and rows.

For example, to delete a row, position the insertion point in the row to be deleted, then select the row using the Table menu's Select Row command and delete it using the Delete Row command.

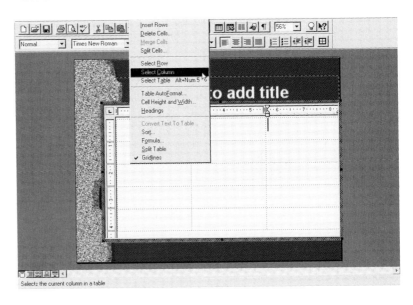

Table Tips

PowerPoint will automatically try to limit the number of rows and columns that you place on a slide. The table layout will be based on the chosen slide size, font, type size, and so forth.

It is possible to change the number and size of rows by using the sizing tools on the vertical and horizontal rulers. And you can insert (copy and paste) tables from Word and Excel documents. Just don't get carried away with 10-column, 20-row tables on a PowerPoint slide. The text will be too small for your audience to read. If possible, experiment with table dimensions using the medium and projection system you plan to employ.

FORMATTING TEXT

While PowerPoint automatically chooses fonts, colors, character sizes, and the like, you can overrule these choices on individual slides and reports or for entire templates. You use toolbars, menu choices, and dialog boxes that will seem familiar from your work with other programs in the Office package.

Aligning Text

You can right-align, left-align, center, or justify text easily. There are toolbar buttons galore just for this purpose. But to really make your audience seasick, the Format menu's Alignment command offers the most options—found on a submenu, as illustrated in Figure 5.2. In any case, start by selecting text, then apply the desired formatting.

Alternatively, you can use the Left-align and Center toolbar buttons, labeled in Figure 5.2.

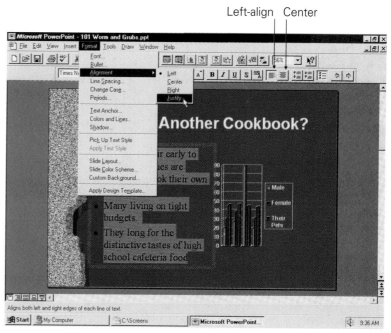

Figure 5.2 First select the text to be aligned, then use the Format | Alignment command or toolbar buttons to align it.

Here too, moderation is called for. PowerPoint does a pretty good job of aligning text all on its own. But excessive white space between justified words bothers some people and wastes valuable slide real estate. You can manually hyphenate words by typing a dash, then SHIFT-ENTER to minimize this waste.

Changing Fonts and Sizes

You have the usual tools at your disposal:

- The Formatting toolbar buttons
- Keyboard shortcuts
- The Format menu's Font command
- The Tools menu's Replace Font command

Select the text of interest and then apply the desired formatting. PowerPoint will tell you if you need to switch views. Let's see some examples of the less obvious formatting choices.

Shadow Effects

Perhaps you've noticed those shadow effects applied by some of the Microsoft AutoFormat features. You can also add them manually. Work in full-size views (choose 100% on the Standard toolbar) to get the best view of the effect:

1. Select the text.
2. Click the shadow button on the Formatting menu for default shadow effects, or choose Shadow from the Format menu.
3. Make your choices in the resulting Shadow dialog box. Usually just a few points of Offset is all that's required.
4. Click OK. You may need to deselect the text to see the results.
5. Experiment with different amounts of Offset.

Embossing Text

Select the text and choose Emboss from the Font dialog box.

**habits &
strategies**

Moderation is a good thing

when applying shadows.

Nobody likes a show-off, and

too much shadow effect makes

text difficult to read.

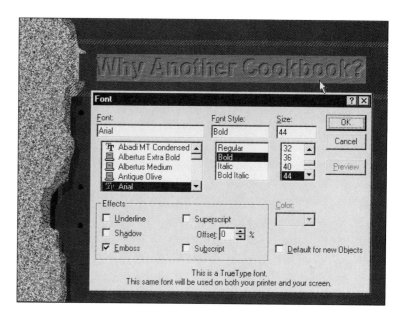

SHORTCUT

Underline and most other formatting commands toggle; reapplying them on previously formatted text removes the formatting.

Underlining Text

To underline text, select it and use the Formatting toolbar's Underline button or the CTRL-U keyboard shortcut. You can also apply underlining from the Font dialog box.

You may notice that the Underline feature in PowerPoint uses a continuous underline by default (that is, it includes the spaces and any punctuation between words). To underline single words, you must select and underline them one at a time.

In the Colors dialog box, you can either choose a color shown or create your own by clicking the Custom tab.

Font Colors

Here are the steps to changing the color of text in PowerPoint:

1. Select the text.
2. Either click the Text Color button and then click the desired color in the palette, or choose Font from the Format menu.

3. In the dialog box that appears, click on the Color list arrow.
4. Choose one of the basic colors shown on the palette or choose Other Color.
5. If you chose Other Color, click on the desired color in the Colors dialog box.

habits & strategies

Picking the wrong colors for slides and overheads can make them illegible. That's why PowerPoint offers to make color choices for you. If you plan to get creative, test your work using the output device and preferably the projection system you plan to use in your final presentations.

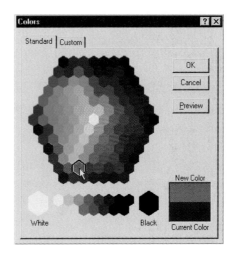

6. Click OK to close the Colors dialog box.

7. Click OK in the Font dialog box to finish up.

8. You may need to deselect the text to experience the resulting show of color.

Incidentally, you need not have a color display to use color. If you plan to print your output on a color printer, or send files out to a slide-making company, you can specify colors on your black-and-white screen and get color output.

Changing Case

PowerPoint lets you change the case of selected text. For instance, you can switch all text to upper case, or automatically create "capitalized" sentences. Use Change Case command on the Format menu to do this. The resulting dialog box illustrates the effect of each available choice (including the rather interesting "tOGGLE cASE").

Alas, there is no Small Caps option; and this feature cares not a whit about the content of your document. So if you select a sentence containing acronyms like ASAP, you'll end up with things like asap or Asap. Check your work.

Replacing One Font with Another

When you change design templates, PowerPoint automatically picks fonts for you. You can also choose fonts on your own by using the Replace Fonts command on the Tools menu.

1. Choose the Replace Fonts command on the Tools menu. The Replace Font dialog box will appear.

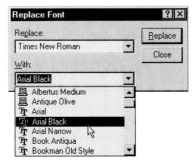

2. Choose the font that you wish to replace from the drop-down list, or type the font name.
3. Choose the replacement font from the second list, or type its name.
4. Click Replace.
5. Close the Replace Font dialog box.

What a Country! Check your slides; you may need to reformat some things (perhaps enlarge a title or body object here and there, or tighten line spacing to make things fit). If you hate the results, just replace the new font with the old font and try something else.

Line and Paragraph Spacing

You can change the amount of space between lines and before and after paragraphs in body objects and title objects. You can change all of the paragraphs in a text object, or just selected lines.

1. Switch to Slide view if you are not already there.
2. Select the line(s) or text object(s) you wish to reformat.
3. Choose Line Spacing from the Format menu.
4. Use the Line Spacing dialog box to specify new settings in either lines or points.

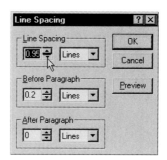

5. Click Preview to see the effect of your choices.
6. Click OK to make the changes.

Copying Text Styles

There are two ways to copy text formatting. One uses the Pick Up and Apply commands on the Format menu; the other uses a toolbar button.

To copy text formatting with the menu commands:

1. Select the text containing the formatting you'd like to copy.
2. Choose Pick Up Text Style from the Format menu.
3. Select the text you wish to reformat.
4. Choose Apply Text Style from the Format menu. (This choice is visible only after you've picked up some formatting.) The selected text will be reformatted.

If you don't select multiple words for reformatting, only the word containing the insertion point will be reformatted.

To use the Format Painter button on the Standard toolbar:

1. Select the text containing the formatting you want to copy.
2. Drag across the Format Painter button. It looks like a paintbrush.

Learn more about importing and exporting (and the PowerPoint Pack and Go Wizard) in Chapter 12.

3. The mouse pointer changes shape. (It will look like a paintbrush, too.)

4. Click the text you wish to reformat. The selected text will be reformatted.

IMPORTING TEXT

PowerPoint can import text from a surprising number of other programs. For example, you can open a Microsoft Word document using PowerPoint's Open command and PowerPoint will convert the document into a PowerPoint presentation (an outline, actually) that you can format into pleasing slides, then save the results as a PowerPoint document.

Text formatted with the *heading 1* style from your Microsoft Word document becomes a slide title, a *heading 2* becomes the first level of text, and so on. If the document contains no styles, PowerPoint uses the paragraph indentations to create your outline. In plain text documents, PowerPoint uses tabs at the beginning of paragraphs to define the outline structure.

You can also import text from other word processors, tables from Microsoft Excel worksheets and elsewhere. To learn more, check the online Help topic "import."

upgrade note

PowerPoint's new Style Checker can really make your presentations look great. Take a few moments to read about it!

STYLE CHECKER ASSURES CONSISTENT PRESENTATIONS

PowerPoint's new Style Checker will help you make certain that your spelling is correct and that the little details like capitalization and periods are consistent. You begin by choosing Style Checker from the Tools menu.

The command opens a dialog box that lets you define the checks to be made. Clicking the Options button in that dialog box gives you control over the checker's parameters. Let's take a look at your options.

You can reach the spelling checker either via the Spelling command in the Tools menu or by enabling spell checking as part of Style checking in the Style Checker dialog box.

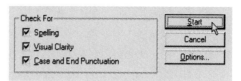

Spell Checking

PowerPoint's spelling checker dialog box should look familiar if you have ever used Microsoft Word or Excel. The PowerPoint spelling checker shares dictionaries with your other Microsoft Office applications (if you have installed Microsoft Office properly). PowerPoint's spelling checker doesn't, however, let you check just selected parts of your presentation. It always checks all of the words in your slides, notes, and other printouts—with two important exceptions: It will *not* check words in your drawings and other graphics, and it does not "spell check" filenames.

You can work in Outline or Slide view when checking spelling. To start the checker, press F7, use the Standard toolbar button, or choose Spelling in the Tools menu. The checker will scan your whole presentation looking for unfamiliar words (unrecognized collections of text surrounded by spaces, actually). When it finds one, it will highlight it in your presentation and place it in the Not In Dictionary section of the Spelling dialog box, as shown in Figure 5.3.

You can accept PowerPoint's suggestions, type a correction of your own, add the unfamiliar word to a custom dictionary, or skip the word by clicking the appropriate buttons. When making changes, you can have PowerPoint always make the same correction without asking you again in the same spell-checking session.

Visual Clarity

The Visual Clarity checker assures that you don't gunk up a presentation with too many typestyles, too many bullets per slide, the

habits & strategies

Run the checker after you've entered all of your text but before doing your final formatting, and before changing Design Templates, and so forth, since some corrections will change line endings, affecting the amount of room available on a slide, and so on.

Unfamiliar words are highlighted
and appear in the dialog box

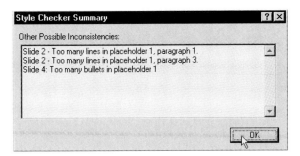

PowerPoint shares your other
Office dictionaries

Figure 5.3 The spelling check highlights unfamiliar text strings and offers suggestions.

wrong type sizes, text accidentally positioned off the edges of slides, and so forth. It will warn you of these and other problems.

To change the rules, use the Options button in the Style Checker dialog box and visit the Visual Clarity tab:

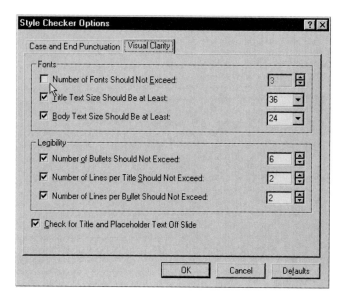

Case and End Punctuation

If you are like me, you can never decide whether or not to end each bullet list item with a period. Sometimes you capitalize, sometimes you don't. Or perhaps you are combining the works of multiple authors with different styles. Fortunately, the Case and End Punctuation command can help.

1. Finish entering your text.
2. Choose the Style Checker command from the Tools menu.
3. Click the Options button, then choose the Case and End Punctuation tab if necessary to change the options, then click OK.

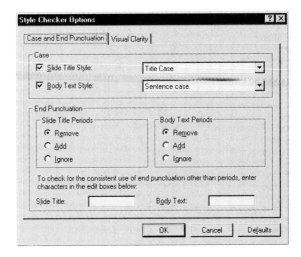

4. Make sure the Case and End Punctuation box has a checkmark.
5. Click Start.
6. PowerPoint will check spelling first if that option was also checked in step 4.
7. The style checker will inform you of inconsistencies and give you the choice of ignoring or fixing them.

Manually Adding and Removing Periods in Sentences

To manually add or remove periods in the sentences in your slides (rather than using the Style Checker) follow these steps:

1. Select the text you wish to conform.
2. Choose Periods from the Format menu.
3. Choose Add Periods or Remove Periods to suit your taste.
4. Click OK.

HEADERS, FOOTERS, DATES, TIMES, AND PAGE NUMBERS

It is possible to include text in the footer (at the bottom) of all or selected slides and handouts. Use this dialog box to specify these

CAUTION

As illustrated in Figure 5.4, you should check your work after using the Remove Periods command. Computers are just dumb servants. They will obediently remove periods even after abbreviations like etc.

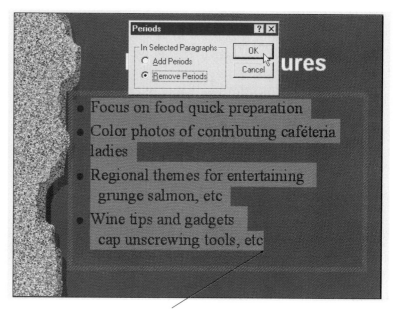

All periods at the end of an item will be removed—including ones at the end of abbreviations

Figure 5.4 You can quickly add or remove periods in selected paragraphs.

options. Watch the preview as you work. (Figures 5.5 and 5.6 show finished headers and footers.)

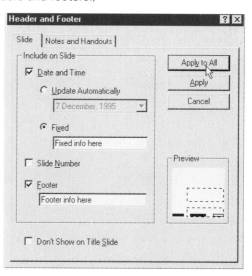

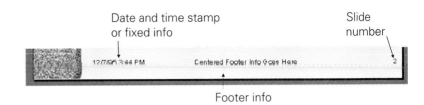

Date and time stamp
or fixed info

Slide
number

Footer info

Figure 5.5 Typical footers

1. Switch to Slide view if you are not already there.
2. Choose the Header and Footer command from the View menu.
3. Click the Slide tab if you are not already there.
4. To insert a date and time that will be automatically updated, make sure there is a check in the Date and Time box. Pick the desired date format from the drop down list. (To print a specific, non-changing date, enter it in the Fixed box instead.)
5. Type desired text in the Fixed box. (It will appear at the left edge of the footer.)
6. If you want slide numbers to appear in the footer, check that option.
7. Type text in the Footer box. (This text will appear in the center of the footer.)
8. To prevent the header from showing on the Title (first) slide, remove the check from that option box.
9. Click the Notes and Handouts tab.
10. Repeat steps 3-5 to specify *headers* on handouts and notes.
11. Specify a footer for handouts if desired.
12. Click Apply to All.

In many layouts you must choose between displaying the time and date or fixed information. They are mutually exclusive.

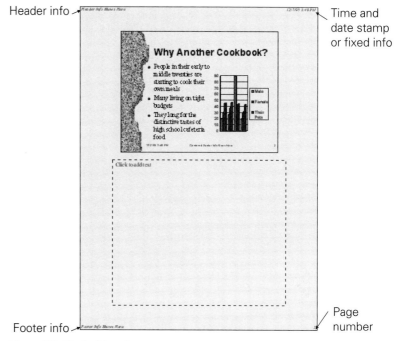

Header info — Time and date stamp or fixed info

Footer info — Page number

Figure 5.6 Typical headers

WHAT'S NEXT?

Now that you are a certified word charmer, it's time to turn our attention to graphics—drawings, photos, and other embellishments that can help keep your audience awake and amazed at your computer prowess. Besides, PowerPoint's graphics tools are fun to use.

6

Working with Graphics

107

FAST FORWARD

SET UP A CLIPART
GALLERY FOR THE FIRST TIME ➤ *pp. 112-113*

1. Choose Clip Art from the Insert menu. You will see a dialog box inviting you to add collections of clip art, with a list of Microsoft art collections.
2. Click to place checkmarks next to the collections you wish to add to the gallery, then click OK.
3. Alternatively, to add all art, click the Add All button. You should see the Microsoft ClipArt Gallery window with your art catalogued.

ADD CLIPART GALLERY IMAGES ➤ *p. 113*

1. Choose Clip Art from the Insert menu.
2. Click the Organize button.
3. Click the Add Pictures button.
4. Locate the picture to add and double-click.
5. Type descriptive key words to help you catalog and locate the image.
6. Click to select categories and/or add new categories.
7. Click OK.

INSERT CLIPART GALLERY
IMAGES IN SLIDES ➤ *pp. 113-115*

2. Click the Insert Clip Art button (on Standard toolbar). You'll see the ClipArt Gallery.
3. Browse categories and images.
4. Double-click on the chosen picture. A copy of the picture will appear on your slide.
5. Drag a sizing handle of the image to change its size.
6. Drag the image itself to reposition it.

USE THE AUTOCLIPART FEATURE ➤ *pp. 116-118*

1. Enter and spell-check all text.
2. Choose AutoClipArt from the Tools menu.
3. When you see the AutoClipArt dialog box, pick a word to illustrate.
4. Click the Take Me to Slide button.
5. Click the View Clip Art button. PowerPoint presents images that might illustrate the specified word.
6. Double-click the image you like the most. The image will be pasted into the slide.

IMPORT AND INSERT
PHOTOS AND OTHER GRAPHICS ➤ *pp. 118-121*

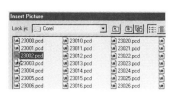

1. Go to the slide needing the image or insert a new slide to receive the image.
2. Use any of these commands: Picture (Insert menu), Clip Art (Insert menu), or Object (Insert menu).
3. Choose the correct type of graphic element (PhotoCD, TIFF, bitmap, and so forth).
4. Double-click the file name of the desired image. PowerPoint will insert a full-size copy of the chosen image.
5. Resize and reposition the graphic as desired.

USE POWERPOINT'S
DRAWING TOOLS ➤ *pp. 121-122*

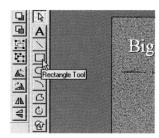

1. Switch to a slide where you want to insert a drawing or insert a new slide.
2. Use the resulting dialog box to choose your favorite object type and related tools (PaintBrush, Word Picture—whatever).
3. Use the drawing toolbar(s) to draw lines, add labels, and so forth.
4. Close the drawing, inserting it in the slide.
5. Resize and reposition if necessary.

USE AUTOSHAPES TO
SPEED DRAWING TASKS ➤ *pp. 122-123*

1. Switch to the slide needing artwork or insert a new slide.
2. Choose Toolbars from the View menu to display the AutoShapes toolbar.
3. Pick a shape from the AutoShapes toolbar (the star, for instance).
4. Drag with your mouse to define the desired size of the chosen graphic.
5. Position the graphic by selecting it and then dragging it.
6. Use the Drawing toolbar's Text Tool to add text, then use the Formatting toolbar to embellish the text, and so forth.
7. Repeat steps 3-6 until finished. Close the drawing to insert it, resize, and reposition as necessary.

The whole point of Windows 95 and monolithic software creations like PowerPoint is to let us express ourselves with something other than our keyboards. "If a picture's worth a thousand words," one advertisement reads, "how come we still use so many words?" I don't remember the name of the product in that ad, but it sure is a compelling headline, isn't it?

In this chapter you'll see how to use free artwork provided by Microsoft, and how to incorporate photos and graphics from numerous other sources. You'll learn how to create your own art with the help of PowerPoint's drawing tools and a gadget called AutoShape. It makes even the most ham-fisted of us look like we went to Art Center (or at least like we took one of those correspondence school art courses). Last, but by no means least is a new PowerPoint feature called *AutoClipArt*. It scans your presentation looking for key words and suggests graphics that might help illustrate or complement the words. Let's get graphical!

definition

Clip Art: *Drawings of people, places, and things used to decorate and illustrate documents, often cartoon-like in appearance. Called clip art because, for decades, this type of art was sold in paperback books. Users clipped out the desired images (destroying the books), and pasted the clipped art into documents.*

THE CLIPART GALLERY

The Microsoft ClipArt Gallery is a program that helps you organize, categorize, preview, and insert graphic files. PowerPoint's very cool *AutoClipArt* feature requires the ClipArt Gallery.

Begin by either choosing Clip Art from the PowerPoint Insert menu or clicking the Standard toolbar's Insert ClipArt button, which reminds me of a red-headed Barney Rubble. (You should be in Slide view and might need to click outside of a text object to undim the Clip Art menu choice.)

With any luck your ClipArt Gallery will already be set up. If it is, you will see miniature previews of graphics (probably cartoonish drawings similar to those in the illustration at the beginning of this topic).

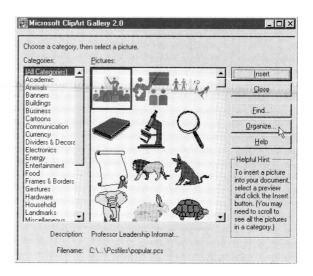

*You need not limit your gallery
contents to images provided by
Microsoft. You can add virtually
any graphics file to the gallery
and categorize it for easy
retrieval.*

Setting Up Your ClipArt Gallery

Fortunately, setup is a pretty simple affair. If the Pictures area of
your Microsoft ClipArt Gallery window is empty, you'll need to locate
and catalog the graphic images on your disk(s). At this point, you might
see a dialog box inviting you to add collections of clip art. There will be
a list of Microsoft art collections that you installed along with Windows,
and perhaps Microsoft Office, and Microsoft Plus!

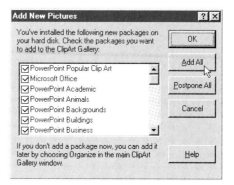

Click to place checkmarks next to the collections you wish to add
to the gallery. (What you are really doing is "cataloging" images already
on your disk and creating miniature preview images, so you are not
squandering a lot of disk space on full-size duplicates.) That's why I vote

for clicking the Add All button. In a moment you should see the Microsoft ClipArt Gallery window with your art catalogued. If not, go to online help for assistance.

ADDING ITEMS TO THE CLIPART GALLERY

It's easy to add additional images to your ClipArt Gallery at any time. Here are the general steps:

1. Choose ClipArt from the Insert menu.
2. Click the Organize button.
3. Click the Add Pictures button.
4. Locate the picture to add and double-click.
5. Type descriptive key words to help you catalog and locate the image.
6. Click to select categories and/or add new categories.
7. Click OK.

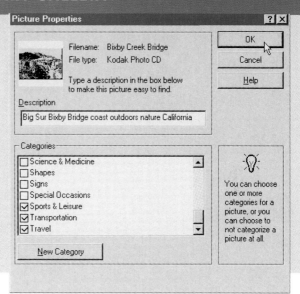

habits & strategies

I keep my photo files and other frequently-used graphic files in a folder called Art. It makes them easy to find when I am in a hurry.

Using Your Gallery

Once the ClipArt Gallery is working, it's easy to use. Suppose we wanted to add some clip art to this slide:

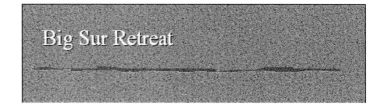

1. After switching to the slide and perhaps dragging the text object's bottom edge up to make room for the graphic on the slide, you could click on the Barney Rubble-looking

Insert ClipArt button on PowerPoint's Standard toolbar. You'll see the ClipArt Gallery.

2. Browse the various categories and images and double-click on the chosen picture. A copy of the picture will appear on your slide:

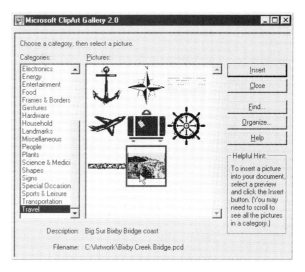

3. Drag a sizing handle to change the object's size, then drag the image itself, if necessary, to reposition it. Here, the image has been resized and repositioned:

4. Later, if you want to substitute a different image from the ClipArt Gallery, simply double-click on the graphic in your slide. This will bring up the Gallery where you can choose a *new* image from the Gallery. Too easy!

Changing Colors in Clip Art

Frequently the colors used in clip art clash with slide backgrounds. Worse still, parts of a graphic occasionally disappear because they are the same color as a slide's background. Help is at hand:

1. Right-click a clip art image in your slide.
2. Choose Recolor from the resulting shortcut menu.
3. Choose the color you wish to change by clicking to put a checkmark in the corresponding box.
4. Pick the desired replacement color from the drop-down list.
5. Change other colors as desired.
6. Click Preview if you are uncertain about the likely results.
7. Click OK when you are happy.

Here's an example of the clip art image used In the preceding example with just the skin tones changed. Pretty slick, huh?

AUTOCLIPART

Well, what if you are too lazy—I mean, too *busy* to browse manually through your clip art collection? The new AutoClipArt feature can help. As you read earlier, it scans your document looking for keywords that match descriptions in the ClipArt Gallery and proposes them as possible works of art for particular slides. Here are the steps with an example of the feature at work:

1. Finish entering and spell-checking all of your text.
2. Choose AutoClipArt from the Tools menu.

3. AutoClipArt will scan your text looking for words corresponding to clip art descriptions.
4. You will soon see the AutoClipArt dialog box.

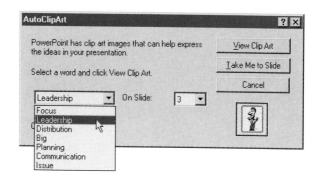

5. Pick a word that you might want to illustrate ("communication" in our example).
6. Click the Take Me to Slide button.
7. PowerPoint will display the slide containing the selected word.
8. Click the View Clip Art button.
9. You will see the ClipArt Gallery dialog box proposing images that might illustrate the specified word.

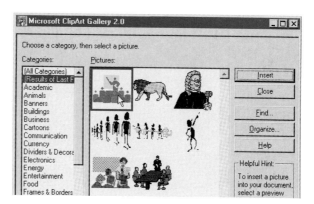

10. Double-click the image you like the most.

11. The image will be pasted into the slide, and you will be returned to the AutoClipArt dialog box where you can either repeat steps 5-11 or close the dialog box (click Cancel or use the close button in the upper-right corner).
12. Revisit the slide(s) containing the new art and resize, reposition, and recolor it to your heart's content.

Here's an example of a finished slide. (I told you this was an intriguing feature!)

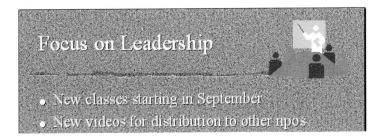

IMPORTING PHOTOS AND OTHER GRAPHIC IMAGES

The general steps for importing, sizing, and positioning images for use with PowerPoint are pretty straightforward. In fact, you saw them at work already earlier in the book. Here they are in a nutshell, with an example:

1. Open the PowerPoint presentation needing a graphic image.
2. Go to the slide needing the image or insert a new slide to receive the image. (Choose either a slide layout specifically designed for graphics or any other.)
3. Use any of these commands: Insert|Picture, Insert|Clip Art, or Insert|Object.
4. Choose the type of graphic element you wish to import, if more than one type is offered (PhotoCD, TIFF, bitmap, and so forth).

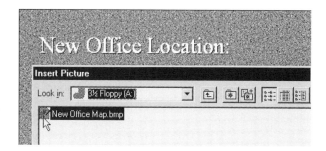

5. Choose the file name of the desired image. (A bitmap, or "Paint" image, in this example.)
6. Click OK and PowerPoint will insert a full-size copy of the chosen image, converting its file format if necessary.
7. Use your mouse to resize and reposition the graphic as desired.
8. To edit the image, you can often (but not always) double-click on it.

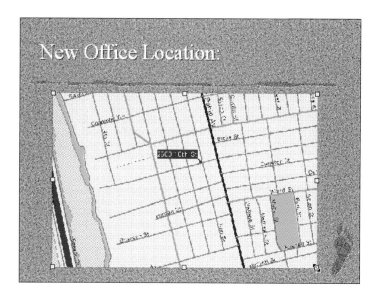

Inserting Photos

You can insert scanned photos into PowerPoint slides, but there are some things you should know. First of all, photos take *lots* of disk

CAUTION

Photos slow down the loading of slides and the process of switching from slide to slide in an electronic presentation, particularly if you are using a slow machine. Rehearse on the machine you'll use for the presentation to see if this will be a problem.

space, particularly if the images are large and in color. This is particularly important to know if you plan to pass around your PowerPoint presentations on floppies.

Large photos can also slow you down when editing a presentation, since it takes time for the photos to be displayed. Consider leaving "holes" where the photos will go, then insert the actual images at the end of your creation process.

Photos may *print* better than they look *on screen* if you do not have a high-resolution monitor. This is not a big problem unless you plan to give on-screen presentations. If you do, consider investing in a high-resolution monitor and display card. Preview before the audience arrives to see what to expect.

It takes a long time to print slides containing photos. Leave yourself plenty of extra time for printing if your presentation has photos. That said, here's how to do it. The process works a lot like inserting other graphics, except that you might have to make some file conversion and resolution decisions:

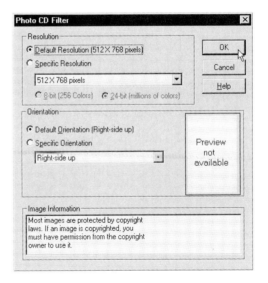

1. Switch to an existing slide and pick Picture from the Insert menu, or start a new slide with a layout with room for a picture.

2. Choose Picture from the Insert menu.
3. Locate and double-click the icon representing the file containing the photo of interest.
4. If you are asked to make decisions about resolution and other settings start with the defaults that PowerPoint suggests unless you know better.

5. Resize and reposition the photo if necessary.

DRAWING IN POWERPOINT

Use the Toolbars choice on the View menu to turn on the Drawing toolbar, Drawing+ toolbar, or both. The toolbars can be reshaped and moved, as is always the case.

You can draw right on slides using the PowerPoint drawing tools. For example, here I've added a white line using the Line tool from the Drawing Toolbar:

Most of the drawing tools and concepts should be familiar to you if you've ever used any Microsoft drawing tools before. Figure 6.1 shows both toolbars and their button functions:

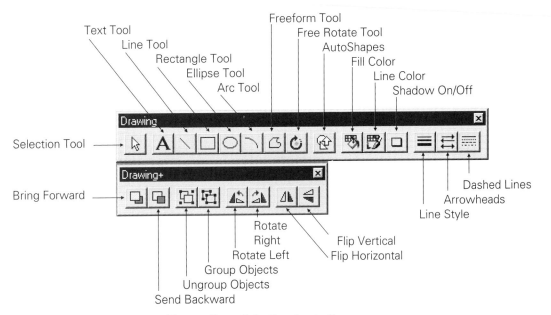

Figure 6.1 The two PowerPoint Drawing toolbars

AutoShapes for Everyday Objects

PowerPoint offers a nifty AutoShapes drawing feature that's worth a look. It's less complicated than Microsoft Paint and combines a small collection of clip art with some text tools. For example, here I've added an arrow and a seal, changed their colors, and used the Semi-Transparent feature in the Colors and Lines options dialog box to make the seal background more interesting.

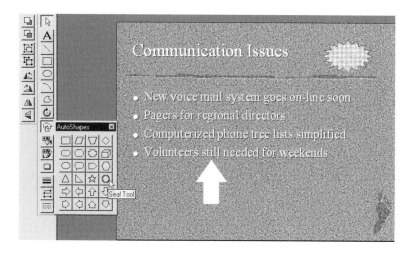

1. Switch to the slide needing artwork or insert a new slide.
2. Choose Toolbars from the View menu to display the AutoShapes toolbar.
3. Pick a shape from the AutoShapes palette (such as an arrow or seal).
4. Drag with your mouse to define the desired position and size of the chosen graphic.
5. Position the graphic by selecting it and then dragging it.
6. Use the Drawing toolbar's Text Tool to add text, then use the Formatting toolbar to embellish the text, if you like.
7. Right-click the object, if you like, for shortcut menus that will let you change colors and more.
8. Resize it if necessary to make things fit by dragging sizing handles.
9. Group the text and graphic if you wish, to make them easier to move simultaneously.
10. Drag the drawn object and/or text objects to move them.

MANUALLY DRAWING SHAPES AND LINES WITH MICROSOFT PAINT

In addition to using the PowerPoint tools for drawing right on slides, you can insert drawn objects created with Microsoft Paint, and even start new objects and launch Paint from within PowerPoint.

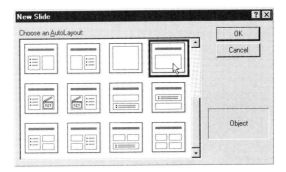

1. Switch to a slide where you want to insert a drawing or insert a new slide. If you use the Insert New Slide command, choose an AutoLayout that includes an object area and double-click in it. (You might need to scroll to see one.)

2. Use the resulting dialog box to choose your favorite object type and related tools (PaintBrush, Word Picture—whatever).

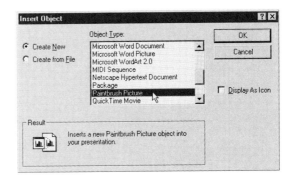

3. When you close the drawing window (by clicking anywhere in the slide), your masterpiece will be inserted into the slide where it can be resized and moved with your mouse.
4. To edit the drawing, just double-click on it.

OBJECT LINKING AND EMBEDDING (OLE)

While space does not permit a lengthy discussion of Object Linking and Embedding (OLE), I should mention that PowerPoint does support the Microsoft OLE standards, and you can insert OLE links to graphics, multimedia, files, and so forth into your slides. For more information about OLE, consult your Microsoft manuals and books like Ralph Soucie's *Making Microsoft Office Work* (Osborne/McGraw-Hill, 1995).

WHAT'S NEXT?

What? Pictures aren't enough? Now you want to add movies and sound to your presentations? Keep reading.

Sounds, Music, and Movies

FAST FORWARD

INSERT A VIDEO ➤ *pp. 130-131*

1. Switch to Slide view.
2. Go to the slide needing a video clip.
3. Choose Insert|Movie to display the Insert Movie dialog box.
4. Locate and double-click on a movie from the list to insert it.
5. Change the animation settings, if desired, by right-clicking (choosing Play is a good idea).

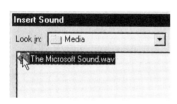

PLAY A VIDEO ➤ *p. 131*

- If the movie object's properties are set to play the clip, simply tap the SPACEBAR when you see the slide containing the video. Otherwise, click on the movie screen and then click the triangular Play button.
- To pause a movie while playing, click the Pause button. Click Stop to stop it.

INSERT A SOUND
OR MUSIC OR MIDI FILE ➤ *p. 132*

1. Switch to Slide view.
2. Go to the slide needing audio.
3. Choose Insert|Sound to display the Insert Sound dialog box.
4. Locate and double-click on a sound file from the list to insert it.
5. Change the animation settings if desired by right-clicking (choosing Play is a good idea).

PLAY SOUNDS OR MUSIC ➤ *p. 132*

- If the sound object's properties are set to play the sound or song, simply tap the SPACEBAR when you see the slide containing the sound icon. Otherwise, click on the sound icon itself and then click the triangular Play button.
- To pause a sound file while playing, click the Pause button. Click Stop to stop it.

Well, busy person, this chapter will encourage you to have much more fun than you probably should. Power-Point will let you insert and play virtually any multimedia file your computer can handle. You can play wave sounds, video clips (a.k.a. movies), MIDI sequences, and more. Multimedia files can play as soon as you switch to a new slide or when you click on button-like objects on your screens. We'll look at the basics of incorporating multi-media objects in this chapter, then explore the finer points of how they relate to "animation" features in Chapter 8.

Incidentally, while Microsoft calls video files "movies," I live near Hollywood where people cringe when they hear the word *movies*, and reserve the word *film* for—well, for images on film. So let's use the term *video* whenever possible instead, since it's more accurate, and I need to "do" lunch in this town when I am not writing. Okay?

WHAT YOU WILL NEED FOR MULTIMEDIA

A full discussion of the minutiae of multimedia is beyond the scope of this book. You might want to check out Windows 95 books (like my *Windows 95 for Busy People*) and the manuals that came with your computer and sound accessories.

But basically, you will need a computer that can play sounds through speakers. And you will need a reasonably fast processor and more or less contemporary display electronics. But then much of this is true for Windows 95 in general, so most of you are probably ready to go.

To make sure your computer's sound capabilities are working, use the Windows Find feature to search your main hard disk (including all subdirectories) for the file specification *.wav, then double-click any of the files it finds. You should hear sound. If you don't hear anything,

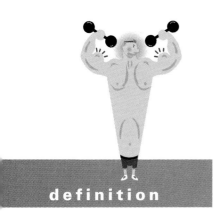

definition

Multimedia Computer: Any annoyingly unreliable, expensive collection of hardware and software connected to cheap speakers. See also: Fun!

check your speaker connection and volume, etc. Get help if this gets too frustrating.

CONSIDERATIONS FOR BUSY PEOPLE

Regular readers of my books probably expect a sermonette at this point, and here it comes. *Anytime you complicate things, they get unreliable, particularly where computers are concerned.* Sound and motion are entertaining, and they definitely have their place in Power-Point presentations. Multimedia can wake up your audience and make you look like a pro.

Over-use of these effects, and the resulting crashes and screeches and freezes, in addition to the waiting for huge multimedia clip files to load can make you look like a real jerk. Furthermore, this multimedia madness takes time to incorporate and test. And, heck, not even Microsoft has thought of all the possible ways you and I can screw this stuff up. So just because it worked during your rehearsal doesn't mean it will work when your boss says, "Hey. Wait a minute. Go back a coupla slides—to the one with the drummer bunny."

Kaboom.

That said, let's have some fun.

If you purchased PowerPoint on a CD-ROM or as part of Microsoft Office, you have some movie files. They end with the extension .mov. Search for them with Windows 95's Find command on the Start menu.

INSERTING VIDEOS IN YOUR POWERPOINT PRESENTATION

If pictures are good, moving pictures must be even better, right? Well, PowerPoint lets you add videos to your presentations to wow people even more. Here are the steps:

1. In Slide view, switch to the slide needing the video or insert a new slide.
2. Choose Insert|Movie to display the Insert Movie dialog box.
3. Double-click a movie from the list to insert it.
4. Right-click on the movie object to bring up the shortcut menu and choose Animation Settings.
5. In the Animation Settings dialog box, in the Play Options list, click on Play (Don't Play is the default). Then click OK.

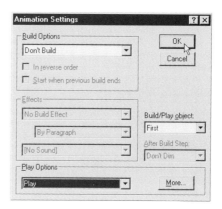

6. Go to Slide Show view to preview your movie.

7. Movies work as if they were extra slides, a lot like a build (discussed earlier). When you reach a slide with a video, press the SPACEBAR or click your primary mouse button to play it (see Figure 7.1).

8. You can stop, pause, or replay the video at any time by using the video controls. You can advance to the next slide by hitting the SPACEBAR or navigate in your slide show using any of the usual techniques.

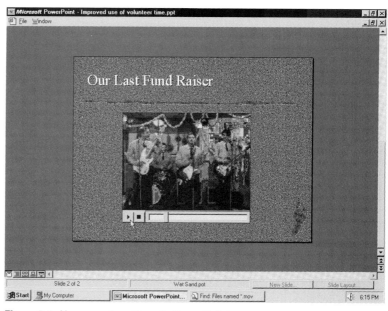

Figure 7.1 You can play videos in PowerPoint.

INSERTING SOUND IN YOUR POWERPOINT PRESENTATION

You can add sound to your PowerPoint slides, in addition to the transition sounds, by following the same steps outlined above for movies. When you get to step 2, just choose Insert|Sounds rather than Insert|Movie. All the other steps are the same.

MIDI AND OTHER SOUND FILES

MIDI files contain instructions that can be used to play the "instruments" built into your sound card or external devices like full-blown keyboards and electronic drum kits. PowerPoint can handle them if your hardware can.

1. Use the Insert|Object command instead of the Insert|Sound command.
2. Select Create from File.
3. Click Browse.
4. Double-click the desired .mid file to insert it into your presentation.

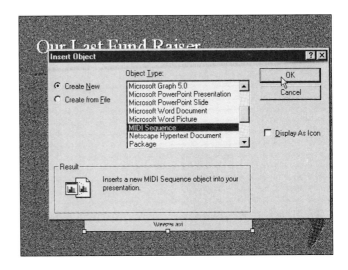

CAUTION

Many (most) multimedia files are copyrighted, and their use is restricted, particularly in profit-related venues. Know your rights and the rights of the files' creators. Get permission when in doubt.

SOURCES OF MULTIMEDIA FILES

The CD-ROM version of Windows 95 comes with numerous multimedia files. If you purchased Microsoft Office or PowerPoint on CD-ROM you'll find more files there. You can find additional multimedia stuff on the Internet, America Online, CompuServe, MSN, ad nauseum. Your sound card probably came with some sample MIDI files, if it is MIDI-capable. Music stores will sell you disks of MIDI files; some of them are killer, others are crap. (Can I write the word "crap" in a computer book?)

You can purchase additional multimedia files at software stores like Egghead, download them online, or you can make your own! Consult your hardware manuals to see how to connect a microphone or other sound source to your computer's audio inputs and record custom sounds. You could even create "self-narrating" PowerPoint presentations, come to think of it.

Those annoying "catalogs on a disc" CDs that keep coming in the mail (and crashing my computer) are often chock-full of great sound and video files. Don't trash them before exploring the possibilities of "lifting" files.

WHAT'S NEXT

OK, busy person, it is time to get back to work. In Chapter 8 you will learn how to polish your presentations.

MAIL

CA

Rearranging
Presentations

135

FAST FORWARD

WORK IN OUTLINE VIEW ➤ *p. 139*

- You can use Outline view for moving, copying, inserting and deleting slides.
- Click the Outline View button at the bottom left of the PowerPoint window or use the corresponding View menu command.
- If all of your slides have titles (a good idea), use the Show Titles button to show just titles.
- If you want to see as many slides as possible simultaneously, specify the minimum permitted percentage in the Zoom Control box on the Standard toolbar (click once on the current view scale and then type **20**).

MOVE SLIDES IN OUTLINE VIEW ➤ *pp. 140-141*

1. Select slides by clicking the slide icons next to slide titles.
2. Drag the little slide icons to move slides. (The mouse pointer becomes a four-headed arrow.)
3. Release the mouse button to move the slide.
4. Undo works here.
5. Slides are automatically renumbered.

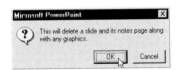

DELETE SLIDES IN OUTLINE VIEW ➤ *p. 144*

1. Select the slide title or titles to be deleted by clicking the slide icons next to slide titles.
2. Press DELETE or use the Cut command or keyboard shortcut (CTRL-X) or the Cut toolbar button to remove a slide. The Cut command replaces the contents of the Clipboard. The DELETE key does not.
3. You will be asked to confirm deletions *only if a slide contains graphics or other non-text elements*. Work carefully. Undo works.
4. Slides are automatically renumbered if necessary.

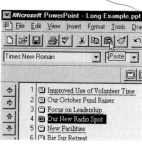

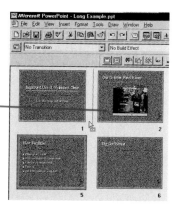

COPY SLIDES IN OUTLINE VIEW ➤ *pp. 141-142*

1. Select the title or titles to be copied while working in Outline view.
2. Use the Copy command or keyboard shortcut (CTRL-C) or the Copy toolbar button to copy a slide or slides. (This replaces the contents of the Clipboard.)

INSERT SLIDES IN OUTLINE VIEW ➤ *pp. 142-143*

1. Copy a slide or slides to the Clipboard with the Copy command (CTRL-C) or the Copy toolbar button. Remember, this replaces the contents of the Clipboard!
2. Click to select the slide just below where you want to insert the slide.
3. Paste slides from the Clipboard with the Paste command (CTRL-V). Or use the Paste toolbar button.
4. The slide is inserted and slides are automatically renumbered as necessary.

WORK IN SLIDE SORTER VIEW ➤ *p. 139*

- Click the Slide Sorter View button at the bottom left of the PowerPoint window or use the corresponding View menu command.
- You can use Slide Sorter view for moving, copying, inserting or deleting slides.
- Specify the minimum percentage in the Zoom Control box on the Standard toolbar (type **20**) if you want to see as many slides as possible, although they will be illegible. Use a larger zoom if you need to read the titles while rearranging slides (a good idea when you don't know slide numbers).

MOVE SLIDES IN SLIDE SORTER VIEW ➤ *p. 141*

1. Select, then drag slide miniatures in Slide Sorter view. (SHIFT-click to select multiple slides, which need not be adjacent.)
2. The mouse pointer becomes a square box with an arrow and a long, skinny "stick" (called the Insertion point). It shows where the slide will be positioned when you release the mouse button. Position the insertion point. (Here slide 5 is being moved to between 1 and 2.)
3. Releasing the button inserts the slide(s) and renumbers the slides as necessary.

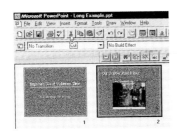

DELETE SLIDES IN SLIDE SORTER VIEW ➤ *p. 144*

1. Select a slide or SHIFT-click to select multiple slides in Slide Sorter view.
2. Press DELETE or use the Cut command or keyboard shortcut (CTRL-X) to remove a slide or slides.
3. You will *not* be asked to confirm deletions. Work very, very carefully. Undo works here!
4. The Cut command replaces the contents of the Clipboard. The DELETE key does not.

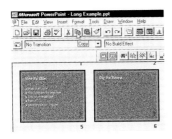

COPY SLIDES IN SLIDE SORTER VIEW ➤ *pp. 141-142*

- Select slide(s) in Slide Sorter view and use the Copy command or copying shortcuts (CTRL-C, etc.) to copy a slide or slides.
- SHIFT-clicking selects multiple slides which need not be adjacent. (Here 5 and 6 are selected.)
- Remember that the Copy command replaces the contents of the Clipboard.

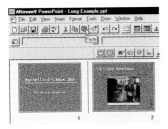

INSERT SLIDES IN SLIDE SORTER VIEW ➤ *p. 143*

1. Click to position the Insertion point between the existing slides where you want to insert the new slide. (Here it will be inserted between 1 and 2.)
2. Paste slides from the Clipboard with the Paste command (CTRL-V) or use the Paste toolbar button.
3. Slides are renumbered If necessary.

DELETE SLIDES IN SLIDE VIEW ➤ *p. 144*

- Click the Slide View button at the bottom left of the PowerPoint window or use the corresponding View menu command.
- Use the Slide view for deleting slides. Display a slide in Slide view and choose Delete Slide from the Edit menu to remove the slide.

Inevitably, you'll need to change the order of slides in your presentation. You'll think of a better sequence of explanations, or some presenter will need to arrive at a different time, or whatever. Maybe you'll decide to delete a slide, or copy one so that you can repeat it elsewhere in your presentation. If you are working with unnumbered 35mm slides or overhead transparencies, and are not using handouts or speakers' notes, you can just shuffle your pile of transparencies or tray of slides and get on with your life.

But if you need the slides in your PowerPoint presentation file to match the order of your presentation for whatever reason, this chapter will explain the process of moving slides from place to place within a presentation file. Incidentally, if you need to know how to move slides from one *presentation* to another, that's covered in Chapter 13.

WHICH VIEW SHOULD YOU USE?

Slide Sorter and Outline views are the two best choices for rearranging the order of slides. Outline view is probably the most efficient, particularly if all of your slides have titles. Slide Sorter view lets you see the non-text elements while you work. Moreover, it's easy to move multiple slides in Slide Sorter view. Some things are not possible or extremely difficult in Slide view. Here's a table of recommended views for each action:

Action	Outline View	Slide Sorter View	Slide View
Move single slides	X	X	
Move multiple slides		X	
Delete single slides	X	X	X
Delete multiple slides	X	X	
Copy slides	X	X	
Insert slides	X	X	

CAUTION

Sometimes Undo can rescue you if you really screw up your presentation's order. Sometimes not. Save your work before rearranging, then check it carefully before saving again!

REARRANGING THE ORDER OF SLIDES

You can rearrange slides by cutting and pasting in Outline or Slide Sorter view but the best way is often to drag slides from place to place. Regardless of which method you use PowerPoint will automatically renumber slides as necessary after you move them around. Let's look at moving slides in Outline view first, then turn to Slide Sorter view.

Rearranging in Outline View

Outline view is nice because you can easily see (and read) the titles of many, many slides at once, and simply drag the slide icons next to each title to rearrange your slides as you can see in Figure 8.1.

Zoom Control (smallest percentage shows most slides)

Current slide numbers (will automatically update)

Drag icons to move slides (notice arrow shape)

Click to show only titles

Click to Show all levels of slide text

Long Horizontal line shows where slide will be dropped (beneath the line)

Outline View button

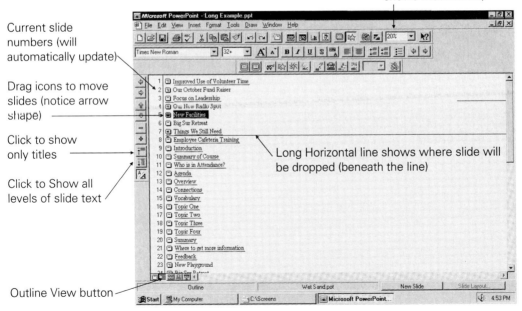

Figure 8.1 Rearranging Slides in Outline View

To move a slide, simply point to its little slide icon and drag. (The mouse pointer will change initially to a four-headed arrow when you point properly, and then to a two-headed arrow when you are dragging properly.) A long horizontal line indicates where the slide will be dropped if you release the mouse button. Releasing the mouse button positions the slide *beneath* that long horizontal line.

The actual number of readable slides that will fit on your display varies with the size of your display, the number of toolbars displayed, the font used for headings, and, of course, your eyesight. Changing the Zoom percentage in the Standard toolbar increases or decreases the size of the characters, therefore increasing the number of slides displayed. Bigger percentages make for bigger words, but fewer titles in view at any one time.

It is possible to cut and paste slides if you prefer not to drag them. The processes of cutting, deleting, and pasting (inserting) are described later in this chapter.

Rearranging in Slide Sorter View

Slide Sorter view is the electronic equivalent of a table top. You can see your slides and quickly change their order. The advantage is you can see all the graphic elements, multimedia icons, colors, and so forth. The bad news is you won't get as many slides on the screen, which can be a nuisance when working on long presentations. And, if you make the slides too small, you won't be able to read their titles. Slides are automatically renumbered after being moved. Figure 8.2 shows a typical Slide Sorter view.

You can SHIFT-click to select multiple slides, but if they are non-adjacent slides, their location after moving can be a little perplexing. Check your work carefully.

COPYING SLIDES

There are many reasons to copy slides. For example, you might want to change just a few items on otherwise identical slides or on a series of slides.

You can copy one slide or multiple slides to the Clipboard in either Outline or Slide Sorter views by using the selection techniques pre-

The disadvantage of rearranging in Outline view is that you can't see graphics and other non-text elements. For that, switch to Slide Sorter view.

SHORTCUT

While in Slide Sorter view, to enlarge a slide for easier viewing (or to edit the slide), double-click it. This switches you to Slide view. Click the Slide Sorter View button to return to the slide sorter.

Zoom Control (smaller numbers display more, smaller slides)

Click to select a slide, SHIFT-click multiple slides

Dark outline(s) indicates selected slide(s)

Drag selected slide(s) to move (notice new mouse pointer shape)

Vertical line shows where slide(s) will be dropped if mouse button is released

Slide Sorter View button

Figure 8.2 Slide Sorter View

viously described, then executing the Edit menu's Copy command or the CTRL-C keyboard shortcut. Remember that when you copy, the prior contents of the Clipboard are lost.

INSERTING SLIDES

Outline view is a handy place to insert, since it's easy to see so many slides (particularly if you only show slide titles). Here's how it works.

Once you have copied a slide or slides to the Clipboard, you can insert (paste) them elsewhere in your presentation. Here are the general steps for inserting while in Slide Sorter and Outline views.

Inserting in Outline View

1. Copy a slide or slides to the Clipboard with the Copy command (CTRL-C). Remember, this replaces the contents of the Clipboard!

2. Click to select the slide just above where you want to insert the slide.

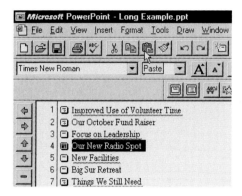

3. Paste slides from the Clipboard with the Paste command (CTRL-V).
4. Slides are inserted and slides that follow the insertion are automatically renumbered as necessary.

Inserting in Slide Sorter View

1. Click to select the slide just *before* where you want to insert the slide(s).
2. Paste slides from the Clipboard with the Paste command (CTRL-V).

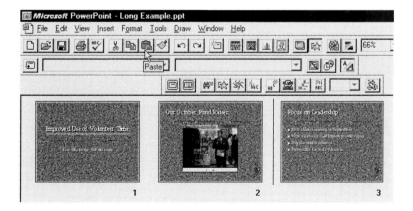

3. Slides are renumbered if necessary.

It is possible to copy slides from one presentation to another using the copying and inserting techniques described here. The inserted slides take on the formatting of the destination presentation. See Chapter 13 for details.

INSERTING BLANK SLIDES

It's often a good idea to place a blank slide at the beginning and end of your presentations, particularly if you plan to give electronic presentations. Here are the steps:

1. Switch to Slide Sorter view.
2. Click to position the vertical insertion point either before the first slide or after the last slide.
3. Click the New Slide button.

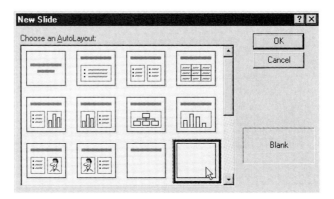

4. Double-click the Blank AutoLayout icon.

DELETING SLIDES

Deleting slides might even be *too* easy. Simply select a slide or slides in Outline or Slide Sorter view. Tap DELETE. In Slide view you can delete the current slide with the Delete Slide command on the Edit menu. In any case the deletions are seemingly instantaneous. Poof. Gone. Vanished. Outta there.

You won't see one of those annoying "Are you really, really sure you wanna delete all those slides?" warning here, busy person. (Yet another reason to be careful what you wish for.)

Undo works if you are on top of things. If not, you'd better hope you've saved recently or have a backup.

CAUTION

You are not asked to confirm the deletion of slides in Slide Sorter view, and you are only prompted in other views when a slide contains non-text elements such as graphics or multimedia clips. Undo will work, but be careful!

WHAT'S NEXT?

On that happy note, let's turn our attention to creating handouts and notes. Timmberrrr!

Printing

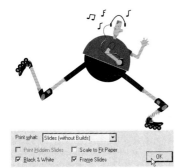

FAST FORWARD

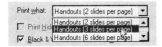

PRINT TRANSPARENCIES OR
SLIDE HANDOUTS (ONE PER PAGE) ➤ *pp. 155-156*

1. Open the presentation.
2. Add any necessary header and footer information.
3. Spell and style check.
4. Load printer with transparency material (or paper).
5. If you are in Slide view, simply click the Print Button on the Standard toolbar.
6. To print from other views, or to print only selected slides, use the File menu's Print command instead of completing step 5.

PRINT MORE THAN ONE
SLIDE PER HANDOUT PAGE ➤ *pp. 156-157*

1. Open the presentation.
2. Add any necessary Header and Footer information.
3. Spell and style check.
4. Choose the File menu's Print command.
5. Specify the slides per page from the Print what drop down list.
6. Specify the range of slides or All.
7. Specify Black and White, framing, or other printing options.
8. Click OK.

PRINT SPEAKER'S NOTES ➤ *pp. 157-158*

1. Open the presentation.
2. Add any necessary header and footer information.
3. Spell and style check.
4. Choose the File menu's Print command.
5. Specify Notes Pages from the Print what drop-down list.
6. Specify the range of slides (and therefore notes), or All.
7. Specify Black and White, framing, or other printing options.
8. Click OK.

PRINT OUTLINES ➤ *pp. 158-159*

1. Open the presentation.
2. Add any necessary header and footer information.
3. Spell and style check.
4. Display the level of detail you wish to print (just slide titles or all text, and so forth).
5. If you are in Outline view, simply click the Print button on the Standard toolbar.
6. To print from other views, or to print only selected pages from the outline, use the File menu's Print command instead of completing step 3.

SPECIFY COLOR OR BLACK
AND WHITE PRINTING ➤ *p. 153*

Use the Black and White printing option checkbox in the Print dialog box (reached with the File menu's Print command).

ABORT PRINTING ➤ *pp. 159-160*

1. Visit the Printer icon for the printer doing the printing (via the Start menu or My Computer window).
2. Select the job or jobs to kill.
3. Choose Cancel Printing from the Document menu.

(As a shortcut, you can cancel the current print job by choosing Print from the File menu and clicking the Stop Print button in the resulting dialog box.)

If you always use your computer's display to give your presentations, you can probably skip this chapter. But chances are, you'll want to print copies of slides to use as handouts, or to mark up while you are perfecting the presentation. And you might find it useful to have speaker's notes and a copy of your outline, even if you always give video-based presentations. Finally, if you plan to make your own overhead transparencies, you'll need to know how to print them. That's all covered in this chapter.

GENERAL PRINTING REMINDERS

Printers (even with the same model number) vary wildly in their capabilities. Some have problems printing accurate colors and acceptable shades of gray. Many will not permit you to print at the extreme edges of pages. A few have trouble printing overhead transparency material, or specific *brands* of transparency material. Some laser printers restrict the number of fonts you can use at any one time. Printing can be painfully slow with some printer and layout combinations.

For all of these reasons, it is very important to test your printer with the design and supplies you intend to use for the final printing of your transparencies, notes, and handouts. Since printing is often the very last step in a hectic meeting preparation schedule, it is a very good idea to test *early* in the project, so that you can make any changes to your layouts, choose different colors, design templates, and so forth *before* the hush falls over your audience.

Incidentally, once printed, overhead transparencies can look terrific on one brand of projector and awful on another, so this is another thing to test.

SHORTCUT

Black and white printing is usually quicker (and cheaper on many color printers). Be sure to use it for drafts if you are only worried about text.

HEADER AND FOOTER REMINDER

PowerPoint lets you place repetitive information at the tops and bottoms of whatever you print (company name, presentation name, dates, times, slide numbers, and so forth). To specify this header and footer information, use the Header and Footer command on the View menu. See Chapter 5 for details.

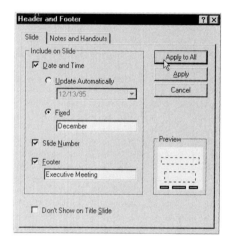

THE POWERPOINT PRINT DIALOG BOX

Since the PowerPoint Print dialog box is a little different from those in other programs, it's worth a visit. Take a look at Figure 9.1.

You display the Print dialog box by choosing Print from the File menu or using the CTRL-P keyboard shortcut. Oddly, if another job is being printed (even with Windows 95's Background Printing feature enabled) you won't be able to see this dialog box until printing is finished.

Printer Information

The Printer information area illustrated in Figure 9.1 should look familiar if you've used other Microsoft programs. The Properties button lets you change printer settings, and takes you to different looking dialog boxes based on your printer's features. Keep the default options whenever possible. See your printer's manuals for details.

CAUTION

The Print button on PowerPoint's Standard toolbar does not take you to the Print dialog box. It starts printing based on the current view. It's a pain to stop printing, so only use the button if you understand its schizophrenic personality described in this chapter.

Specifics of current printer

Click to specify a different printer
if you have more than one

Specifies the range of slides
even when printing outlines

Click to change
printer properties

Specifies type of output
(slides, handouts, etc.)

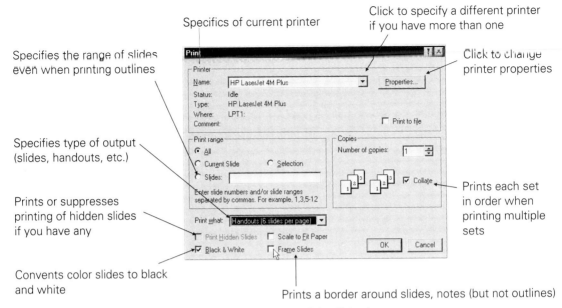

Prints each set
in order when
printing multiple
sets

Prints or suppresses
printing of hidden slides
if you have any

Convents color slides to black
and white

Prints a border around slides, notes (but not outlines)

Figure 9.1 The PowerPoint Print dialog box.

Print Range

The Print range area of the dialog box shown in Figure 9.1 refers to *slides* rather than pages, even when you are printing an outline. That is to say, if you wanted to print all slides or all notes or the complete outline, you would select the All choice. To print just slides three, six, and nine, or just the portions of notes, handouts, or your outline dealing with those three slides, you would type **6,3,9** in the Slides box. To print a continuous range of slides, use a dash. For example, **1-10** would print the first ten slides.

You can also click or SHIFT-click to select slides in Slide Sorter and Outline views, then print just the selected material. After you've selected the slides, use the Selection option in the Print Range section of the dialog box shown in Figure 9.1 to accomplish printing.

Print What

The Print what area of the Print dialog box (illustrated in Figure 9.1) is often the most confusing to new PowerPoint users. Choices you make in the drop-down list determine what prints, and even alters the available choices in the rest of the dialog box. We will examine these choices in more detail throughout the rest of the chapter. Incidentally, to learn more about builds (the process of revealing lines in your slide one at a time), visit Chapter 11.

Print Hidden Slides

As you will see in Chapter 11, you can hide slides and only display them if you need them. If you have hidden any slides in the current presentation, the Print Hidden Slides checkbox shown in Figure 9.1 will be undimmed and let you specify the printing or suppression of hidden slides.

Black and White

The Black and White option removes shading from slides that might make it difficult to read slides printed on black and white printers. Incidentally, you can preview the effect of this feature in Slide and Sorter views by using the Black and White choice on the View menu.

Frame Slides

The Frame Slides choice illustrated in Figure 9.1 causes PowerPoint to print a black line around slides when printing just slides or slides on note pages. It does not add lines to outlines.

Scale to Fit Paper

The Scale to Fit Paper choice matches the slide to the selected paper size and orientation. It is also affected by the settings in the Slide Setup command reached from the File menu.

Copies Settings

Finally, the Copies settings (also illustrated in Figure 9.1) let you specify multiple sets of handouts or slides or whatever. To print multiple copies of complete booklets in the correct order, dial in the desired number of copies and place a check in the Collate box. PowerPoint will print one complete set, then another set, and another, and so on.

Learn Your Printer's Paper Handling Quirks

The collate feature just described and transparency material loading need to be in harmony with your printer's delivery method. That is to say, some printers plop the sheets into the tray face up, others face down. Face up plopping can cause pages to pile up in *reverse order*. When this happens, page ten of a ten-page presentation will be on top, page nine underneath it, and so on. Sometimes, changing a printer lever or electronic setting can change this.

To quickly test a new printer to see if this is a problem, experiment by printing just a couple of copies of a three-page black and white presentation. Check your printer manuals for assistance.

Some transparency materials can only be imaged on one side or the other, so read the box carefully. Usually one-sided materials have a corner notch or other orientation gimmick described on the box or in an enclosure. To make life even more interesting, some printers deposit images on the top side of whatever you dump in the paper tray, others the bottom side. Mine does *one thing* to supplies in the lower tray and the *opposite* to things in the flip-out multipurpose tray. If you attempt to image the wrong side of some materials, the toner will not stick (or worse), so test before you waste a bunch of expensive slide material. This is also an issue with some ink jet printers.

The dilemma of "which side is up" approaches rocket science, so take your time. Figure it all out by writing an X on the top of one side of a sheet of paper and loading it into your printer tray. (Remember if the X was face up or face down and at the back or the front of the printer.) Print something on the test sheet. See if the X comes out on top or bottom and if the printing is on the side with the X. Scratch your head. Is the X laying at the front or back of the printer now? Pace. Talk to yourself. Doodle. It will come to you. If you have multiple trays, repeat the process using a new sheet each time. When you figure it all out, write down the recipe for later reference.

PRINTING TRANSPARENCIES

Your printer might need you to hand-feed transparency material. Some printers will let you just dump a batch into the paper tray and print

CAUTION

Make sure you use transparency material rated for your printer model. Some materials are too thick, too thin, or will melt when passing through your laser printer's hot fuser area (and I can tell you from experience that this is a mess you'll not want to deal with)!

normally. Read the supply boxes before you buy, then experiment. Tape notes to the box once you know the recipe. That said, here are the general steps for printing overheads:

1. Open the presentation.
2. Add any necessary header and footer information.
3. Spell and style check.
4. Load the printer with transparency material (or hand feed if necessary).
5. If you are in Slide view, simply click the Print Button on the Standard toolbar.
6. To print from other views, or to print only selected slides, use the File menu's Print command instead of completing step 5.

PRINTING SLIDE COPIES ON PAPER

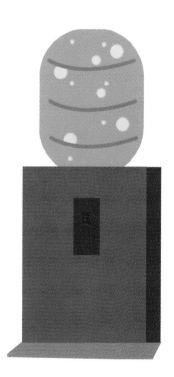

You can print copies of your slides on paper, one slide per page, or you can print reduced sized copies of multiple slides per page. We'll look at one slide per page first.

Printing One Slide Per Page

To print slide copies on paper (one slide per sheet) follow the same general steps as for printing transparencies, except perhaps for specifying multiple copies, collated or not:

1. Open the presentation.
2. Add any necessary header and footer information.
3. Spell and style check.
4. Load the printer with paper.
5. If you are in Slide view, or Slide Sorter view, to print a single copy of all slides (including multiple copies of slides when there are builds), simply click the Print button on the Standard toolbar.
6. To print from other views, or to print only selected slides, or to specify multiple copies of slides, or to specify single

As is often the case in Windows programs, the Print button on PowerPoint's Standard toolbar behaves differently in various views. When in Outline view it prints the outline. In Slide view it prints all of your slides, one per page. In Slide Sorter view, slides print six per page.

slides when there are builds in your presentation, use the File menu's Print command instead of completing step 5. Or, use the CTRL-P keyboard shortcut or choose Print from the File menu.

Printing More Than One Slide Per Page

The best way to print reduced copies of multiple slides per page is to use the desired choice in the Print what section of the Print dialog box:

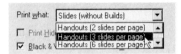

You can choose 2, 3, or 6 slides per page. Frequently, six per page will look just fine, particularly if the slides are not too detailed. This will vary with your design, printer quality, and content. Experiment. Here are the general steps:

1. Open the presentation.
2. Add any necessary header and footer information.
3. Spell and style check.
4. Choose the File menu's Print command.
5. Specify the slides per page (2, 3, or 6) from the Print what drop-down list.
6. Specify the range of slides or All.
7. Specify Black and White, framing, or other printing options.
8. Click OK.

Figure 9.2 shows a typical page of slide handouts.

1 📄 **101 Worm and Grub Recipes**

   A cookbook full of insider tips from notorious school cafeteria ladies...

2 📄 **Why Another Cookbook?**

   - People in their early to middle twenties are starting to cook their own meals.
   - Many living on tight budgets.
   - They long for the distinctive tastes of high school cafeteria food

3 📄 **Key Book Features**

   - Focus on quick food preparation
   - Color photos of contributing cafeteria ladies
   - Regional themes for entertaining
     (grunge salmon, etc.)
   - Wine tips and gadgets
     (cap unscrewing tools, etc.)

4 📄 **Book Outline**

   - Part I   The basics of food buying
   - Part II   Meals as fast as a Green Day Video
   - Part III Just the two of you and a candle
   - Part IV Mushrooms... friends or foes?
   - Part V   Coping with food poisoning
   - Part VI Getting the folks to take you out
   - Part VII Getting a date to take you out

5 📄 **A Typical Reader**

6 📄 **The Video**

7 📄 **Action Items**

   - Ask Randy about the contract.
   - Reorganize last half of book

Figure 9.2 A typical handout page.

SHORTCUT

Place a shortcut for your printer on your Windows 95 desktop or in the top level of your Start menu to quickly reach the print queue. See my Windows 95 for Busy People *book to learn how to do this.*

PRINTING SPEAKER'S NOTES

Speaker's notes are copies of slides with... you've got it, notes for the speaker. Here's an example:

Tell them about the band

Remind them to think about doing the next one outdoors

Tell the bus driver joke

They always print one slide per page. The general steps are simple:

1. Open the presentation.
2. Add any necessary Header and Footer information.
3. Spell and style check.
4. Choose the File menu's Print command.
5. Specify Notes Pages from the Print what drop-down list.
6. Specify the rage of slides (and therefore notes), or All.
7. Specify Black and White, framing, and other printing options.
0. Click OK.

PRINTING OUTLINES

Printed outlines are useful tools for speakers, your audience, or for authors working on a new presentation. You have control over the level of detail printed. Figure 9.3 shows an example of a typical outline page.

Figure 9.3 An outline page.

ABORTING PRINTING REQUESTS

To stop the current printing job, choose the Print command (or click the Print button in the Standard toolbar) and click the Stop Print button:

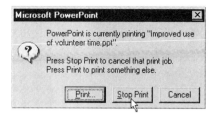

If your printers are shared over a non-Microsoft network (a Novell NetWare installation, for example) your steps for aborting printing might be different. Consult your network documentation or administrator for details.

To kill multiple jobs, use Windows 95's Printers command on the Start menu, pick the printer of interest, and select the job or jobs to be killed. Use the Cancel Printing choice from the Documents menu:

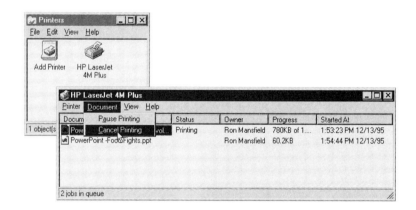

Since most printers have memories that will often contain large portions of your presentation which were sent before you canceled printing, you might need to *reset* the printer to truly "kill" long jobs. (Check your printer manuals to see how this is done.) Just be sure you don't kill wanted printing jobs at the same time!

WHAT'S NEXT?

Chapter 10 describes the process of converting your presentation to 35mm slides. If that's not your output format of choice, skip ahead to Chapter 11 and learn about using computer monitors and other electronic displays for presenting. PowerPoint offers an intriguing collection of video effects, all explored in Chapter 11.

CHAPTER 10

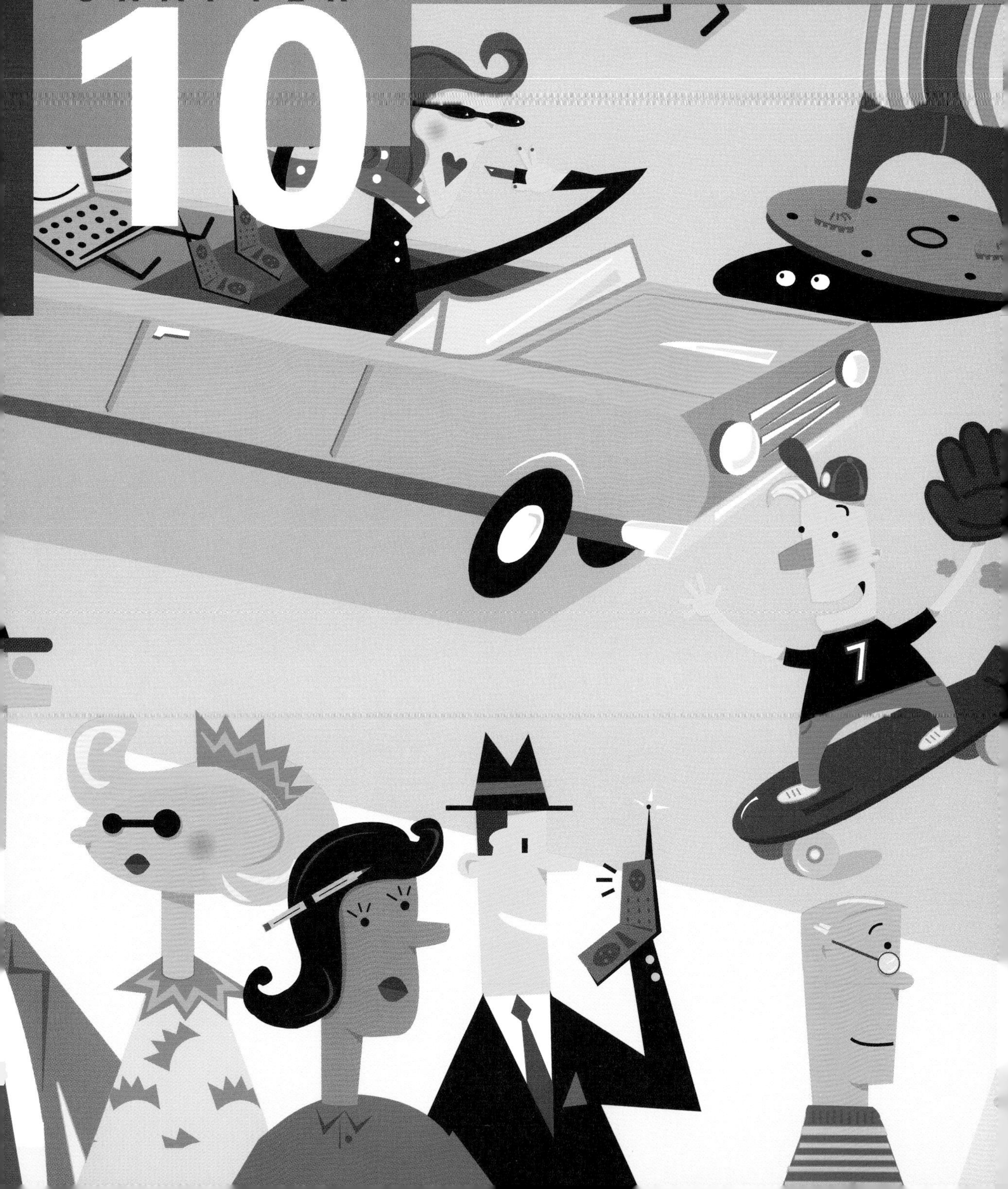

Putting Slides on Film and Posters

FAST FORWARD

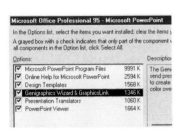

SET SLIDE SIZE ➤ *pp. 166-169*

1. Open the presentation or start a new one.
2. Choose Slide Setup from the File menu.
3. Pick an output type from the Slides Sized for: list or define your own dimensions in the Width and Height boxes.
4. Choose an orientation (Portrait or Landscape).
5. Click OK.

INSTALL GENIGRAPHICS SOFTWARE ➤ *pp. 172-174*

1. Have your Microsoft Office or PowerPoint CD-ROM or diskettes handy.
2. Choose Settings from the Windows 95 Start menu.
3. Choose Control Panel from the submenu.
4. Double-click Add/Remove Programs in the resulting Control panel window.
5. Click the Install/Uninstall tab if necessary to bring it to the top.
6. Double-click either Microsoft Office or PowerPoint.
7. Click the Add/Remove button.
8. If you are installing from a Microsoft Office CD-ROM, select Microsoft PowerPoint and click the Change Option button.
9. Make certain there is a check mark next to the Genigraphics Wizard and GraphicsLink option, then click OK.
10. Follow the onscreen instructions to complete the installation.

USE THE GENIGRAPHICS WIZARD ➤ *pp. 174-179*

1. Inspect your presentation carefully.
2. Have a credit card ready and your modem turned on.
3. Choose Send to Genigraphics from the File menu.
4. Follow the onscreen directions.

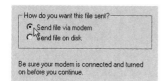

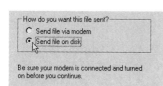

SEND POWERPOINT FILES
TO GENIGRAPHICS VIA PHONE ➤ *p. 176*

1. Make sure your modem is ready.
2. Click Send file via modem in the third Genigraphics Wizard screen.
3. Follow the onscreen directions.

SEND POWERPOINT FILES
TO GENIGRAPHICS VIA DISK ➤ *p. 176*

1. Click Send file on disk in the third Genigraphics Wizard screen.
2. Follow the onscreen directions.
3. Ship your disk(s) to Genigraphics in Memphis, TN.

GET HELP WITH
GENIGRAPHICS PROBLEMS ➤ *pp. 179-180*

1. Open PowerPoint Help.
2. Switch to the Find tab.
3. Type **geni**.
4. Double-click Genigraphics Help in the resulting topic window.
5. Click I have installed Genigraphics, show me the help file.

In the previous chapter you saw how you can use your own printer to create overhead transparencies. These are usually fine for run-of-the-mill meetings, and small to medium size audiences. But when you are presenting to a large group, or when you want to look as professional as possible, it is a good idea to create either 35mm slides or "digital quality" color overhead transparencies. Since the hardware used to create these images is still quite expensive, most of us turn to a service provider like Genigraphics.

In this chapter we will look primarily at Genigraphics, because it is representative of a "full service" house, and because PowerPoint comes with the necessary software to use their facilities easily. Since Genigraphics can also create photographic prints and even posters from your PowerPoint slides, we'll explore those options as well.

CHANGING OUTPUT MEDIA SETTINGS

In order for your presentation to look right, the slides need to have the proper *aspect ratio* for your *output media*. "Huh?" you might be wondering.

Two examples of output media are 35mm slides and 8 1/2" X 11" overhead transparency material. Besides being different sizes, these two media have slightly different aspect ratios. Aspect ratio is a term used to describe the shape of rectangular media—the ratio of the long side to the short side, if you will. Among other things, the aspect ratio of the final presentation's output media determines how many lines you can get on a slide and how long the lines can be.

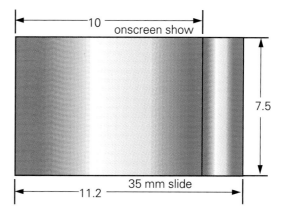

For this reason, the best time to specify the output media is right when you begin creating a new presentation. That's why the Power-Point wizards ask you what type of output you'll be creating. You can, however, go back at any time and change your mind. Here's how:

1. Open an existing presentation or start a new one.
2. Choose Slide Setup from the File menu.

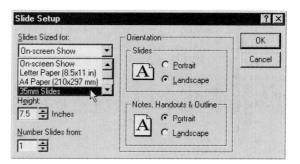

3. Choose the desired output type from the drop down Slides Sized for: list.
4. Pick orientations for slides, notes, and handouts if you don't like the defaults.
5. Click OK.

To see how changing the screen size (and therefore the aspect ratio) changes the appearance of your presentation, check out Figures

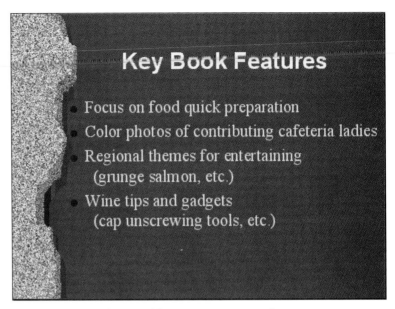

Figure 10.2   A slide formatted for onscreen presentations.

10.1 and 10.2. Figure 10.1 is set for onscreen presentations (the PowerPoint default), and Figure 10.2 is the same slide with 35mm settings. Notice the differing shape of the two slides, and observe how

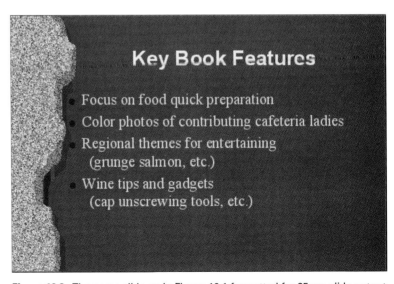

Figure 10.3   The same slide as in Figure 10.1 formatted for 35mm slide output.

close to the edge of the slide the *cafeteria ladies* line is in Figure 10.1, as opposed to Figure 10.2.

OTHER IMPORTANT DESIGN DECISIONS

When you are using a service provider (be it Genigraphics or someone in your home town) there are a number of design factors to consider. These include:

- Fonts used
- Typestyles and other embellishments used
- Type sizes employed
- The resolution used if you scan images into your presentations
- The color palette used
- The color scheme(s) used
- The display color settings used
- The size of your PowerPoint file
- Special characters used (unusual bullets, international accents, and so forth)

For example, Genigraphics officially supports the TrueType fonts shown in Table 10.1. In addition, they support the PostScript fonts shown in Table 10.2.

Algerian (plain)	Anal Black MT	Arial
Arial Narrow	Bookman Old Style	Book Antiqua
Braggadacio	Britannia Bold	Brush Script MT
Century Gothic	Century Schoolbook	Colonna
Courier	Courier New	Desdemona
Footlight MT Light	Garamond MT	Helvetica
Impact	Kino MT	Lucida Fences (plain)
Lucida Arrows (plain)	Lucida Blackletter (plain)	Lucida Bright

Table 10.1 TrueType Fonts Supported by Genigraphics

Lucida Bright Math Extension (plain)	Lucida Bright Math Italic (italic)	Lucida Bright Symbol (plain)
Lucida Calligraphy (italic)	Lucida Extra (plain)	Lucida Fax
Lucida Handwriting (italic)	Lucida Icons (plain)	Lucida Sans
Lucida Typewriter	Lucida Stars (plain)	Matura MT Script Capitals
MS LineDraw	MT Extra	Monotype Corsiva (italic)
Monotype Sorts (plain only)	Times New Roman	Symbol
Wingdings (plain)		

Table 10.1 TrueType Fonts Supported by Genigraphics (continued)

SHORTCUT

If you always use the fonts installed with Windows 95, and the standard choices offered by PowerPoint's design templates, you'll have no font problems with Genigraphics.

If you use fonts other than these in your presentations, you will be warned (by the wizard) when you try to send your presentation to Genigraphics. Not all vendors provide submission software with built-in

Adobe PostScript Fonts	Plain Text	Bold	Italic	Bold Italic
Avante Garde	X	X	X	X
Bookman	X	X	X	X
Courier	X	X	X	X
Helvetica	X	X	X	X
Holvetica Narrow	X	X	X	X
NewCentury Schoolbook	X	X	X	X
Palatino®	X	X	X	X
Symbol	X			
Times	X	X	X	X
ZapfChancery			X	
ZapfDingbats	X			

Table 10.2 PostScript Fonts Supported by Genigraphics

watchdogs like this. And even when you are warned of problems, they can often be solved. For example, if your license permits, you might be able to send copies of the fonts along with your presentation.

Other issues like color palettes and slide orientation (Portrait or Landscape) can be important. Even the resolution used for scanning graphics into your presentations affects the quality of the output. For example, Genigraphics recommends a scanning resolution of 150 dots per inch (or dpi). Other vendors might have other preferences. The moral of the story is: contact your service provider to see what fonts and design features are supported *before* you begin an important project. Many vendors have tip sheets which they can fax to you so that there won't be any surprises when you get your finished slides back. Ask for them.

CHOOSING A SERVICE PROVIDER

As you read earlier, we will be using Genigraphics as the primary example in this chapter, but you should certainly explore alternatives! You might find less expensive service providers locally. To help you get calibrated, consider this: A single 35mm slide from Genigraphics can cost between $7 and $20 (depending on your turn-around time requirements). Add to that the cost of shipping which can be in the range of $20 to $30 and up if you are in a hurry. Genigraphics also charges $0.50 per minute of connect time if you send your PowerPoint file to them via modem. If you send disks instead you will need to pay shipping charges in as well as out. Of course Genigraphics does great work, and they've been around more than 20 years, and price should never be your only consideration.

So, shop around when you are not facing a looming deadline. Run a representative test batch through several places and see what you think. Ask colleagues, particularly when you've seen a great-looking presentation. Computer users groups and their newsletters are also a good source of vendor referrals.

habits & strategies

Test presentations when you are not in a rush, especially if you are using a new vendor.

THE GENIGRAPHICS SOFTWARE

There are two pieces of software that you need if you plan to use Genigraphics. These are the Genigraphics driver, and the GraphicsLink. The driver contains the wizard, adds Genigraphics-specific help files, and makes some changes to your PowerPoint menus. The GraphicsLink software lets you send PowerPoint files via modem.

All of this software might already be installed. To see if it is, go to the PowerPoint File menu and see if there is a choice called Send to Genigraphics. (Don't confuse this with the Send choice, which is something else entirely.) If there is a Send to Genigraphics choice, you can skip to the next section.

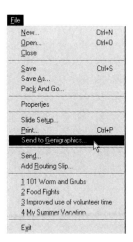

Installing Genigraphics Software

To install the software if it is missing:

1. Have your Microsoft Office or PowerPoint CD-ROM or diskettes handy.
2. Choose Settings from the Windows 95 Start menu.
3. Choose Control Panel from the submenu.

4. Double-click Add/Remove Programs in the resulting Control Panel window.
5. Click the Install/Uninstall tab if necessary to bring it to the top.
6. Double-click either Microsoft Office or PowerPoint.
7. Click the Add/Remove button.
8. If you are installing from a Microsoft Office CD-ROM, select Microsoft PowerPoint and click the Change Option button to see the screen illustration which follows:

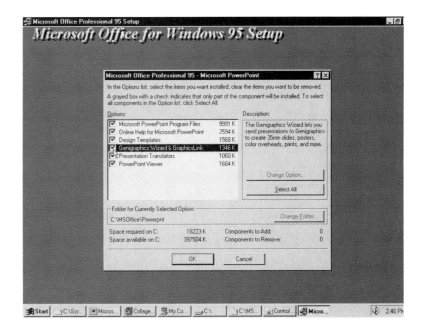

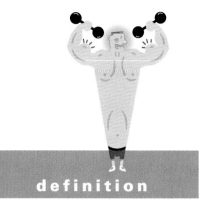

Wizard: Software that leads

you thorough complex tasks,

prompting you for information

as needed.

9. Place a check next to the Genigraphics Wizard and GraphicsLink listing.
10. Click OK.
11. Click Continue.
12. When prompted that the setup was completed successfully, click OK.
13. Close the Add/Remove Programs Properties dialog box.
14. Close the Control Panel.
15. You should see the Send to Genigraphics choice in your PowerPoint File menu.

RUNNING THE GENIGRAPHICS WIZARD

You can send files to Genigraphics either with the Genigraphics Wizard, or by running the GraphicsLink program directly. The Wizard is easier, especially if you are an occasional Genigraphics user, and if you only need to send one presentation at a time.

To run the Wizard:

1. Open the presentation.
2. Make sure the Slide Size setting corresponds to the desired output format (35mm slides, for example).
3. Take a long last look at the content, appearance, and order of the presentation, particularly if you have slide numbering turned on.
4. Style and spell check.
5. Choose Send to Genigraphics from the File menu to see the opening Genigraphics screen:

6. Click Next. You will see a list of available services.

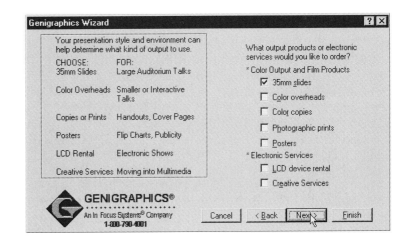

7. Click to choose the one you desire, then click Next.

8. You will be given a chance to choose a different presentation than the current one. Browse to find the different presentation.

9. Select the desired method of sending the presentation. Click Next.

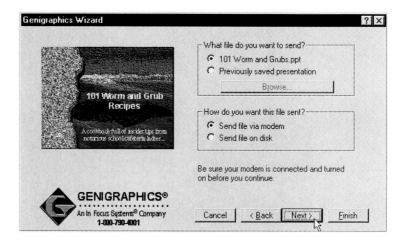

10. You might be asked permission to save the file. Click Yes.

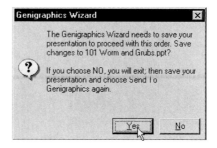

11. You will be presented with options at this point. They will vary according to the type of output media. Here, for example, the wizard wants to know the desired type of 35mm slide mounting. Select the desired options and click Next.

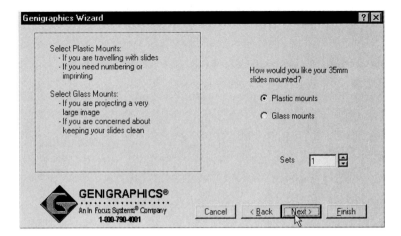

12. Your presentation will be checked for potential problems like unsupported fonts or, as in this example, the wrong slide size settings for the desired output media. You can choose to ignore problems, or see what they will look like if left unsolved (click the Preview button).

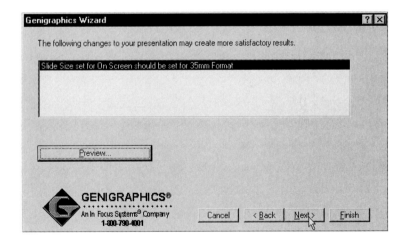

13. More options now, again based upon the chosen media and, to some extent, the contents of the project. Here, for

example, there are no hidden slides so that option is dimmed, but there are slides containing builds. In the illustration which follows, the wizard wants to know if I want one slide with all the elements or an individual slide for each build element (builds are discussed in Chapter 11). Select the desired options and click Next.

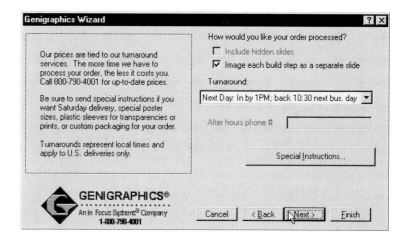

Eventually you will be asked for shipping and billing information (you will need a Visa, MasterCard, or American Express card to use the service). Answer the questions and click Next.

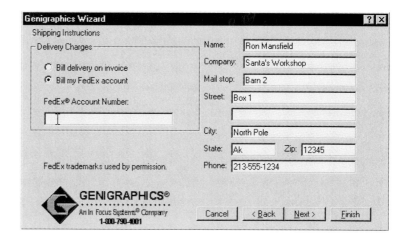

When you click the Finish button, the wizard will dial the phone for you, and with any luck your output will be on your doorstep and your credit card bill inflated as soon as the following morning.

RUNNING GRAPHICSLINK DIRECTLY

If you want a little more control over the process of sending files to Genigraphics, and particularly if you want to send more than one presentation file at a time, you will want to run the GraphicsLink program directly. Start by double-clicking its icon in the PowerPoint (or perhaps MS Office) folder. Follow the onscreen directions or consult online Help.

upgrade note

Be sure you use the right version of GraphicsLink for your current version of PowerPoint. Older versions won't work with the new PowerPoint.

GETTING HELP WITH GENIGRAPHICS QUESTIONS

Speaking of online Help, when properly installed, the Genigraphics software has its own online Help.

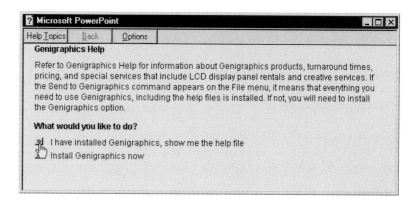

One way to reach the Help file is to:

1. Open PowerPoint Help.
2. Switch to the Find tab.
3. Type **genl**.
4. Double-click Genigraphics Help in the resulting Topic window.
5. Click I have installed Genigraphics, show me the help file.

Genigraphics Phone Support

Genigraphics provides telephone support for their products and services. Reach them at 800-790-4001.

WHAT'S NEXT?

The next chapter will show you how to give onscreen presentations, either for an audience or as a rehearsal tool. Don't miss Chapter 11. It's "must reading."

Preparing and Showing Video Presentations

FAST FORWARD

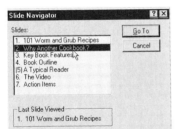

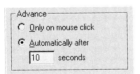

SWITCH TO SLIDE 1 ➤ *p. 188*

- In Slide Show view, press the HOME key, or
- Type **1**, then press ENTER.

GO TO A SPECIFIC SLIDE ➤ *p. 191*

1. In Slide Show view, type the desired slide number.
2. Press ENTER.

(You can also use the Slide Navigator.)

USE THE SLIDE NAVIGATOR ➤ *p. 192*

1. In Slide Show view, right-click anywhere on the screen.
2. Choose Go To.
3. Pick Slide Navigator from the submenu.
4. Double-click the title of the desired slide.

MANUALLY ADVANCE AND BACK UP ➤ *p. 191*

- In Slide Show view, use the left mouse button or press either the SPACEBAR, the RIGHT ARROW, or N to advance slides.
- Click the Left Arrow or press the LEFT ARROW or P key to go back a slide.

AUTOMATICALLY ADVANCE ➤ *pp. 196-197*

1. In Slide Sorter view, click or SHIFT-click to select the slide or slides for which you plan to specify an onscreen time.
2. Click on the Slide Transition button to reveal the Slide Transition dialog box.
3. Click in the box next to the word Seconds and enter the desired onscreen time.
4. Pick a transition effect in this dialog box, if you haven't already.
5. Click OK.

6. Choose View Slide Show.
7. Click the Use Slide Timing option in the Advance section of the dialog box.
8. Click Show.

RUN A SHOW CONTINUOUSLY ➤ *pp. 199-200*

1. Make sure all your slides have transition times assigned to them.
2. Choose Slide Show from the View menu. You'll see the Slide Show dialog box.
3. Select the range of slides to be shown (or use the All default).
4. Select Use Slide Timings in the Advance section of the Slide Show dialog box.
5. Click the Show button.
6. The show will run continuously until you press the ESC key.

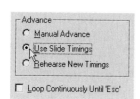

HIDE SLIDES ➤ *pp. 192-193*

1. Switch to Slide Sorter view.
2. Select the slide or slides you wish to hide.
3. Click the Hide Slide button.
4. The slide number or numbers will be covered with gray boxes and a diagonal slash.

To hide slides currently onscreen, press B to replace the slide with a black screen or W to white-out the screen. These keys toggle.

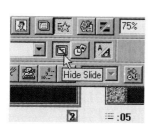

SHOW HIDDEN SLIDES ➤ *p. 193*

- Type the number for a hidden slide and press ENTER, or
- Press H while showing the slide before a hidden slide, or
- In Slide Navigator view, select hidden slides, which are designated by a number in parentheses.

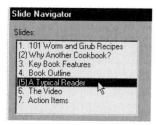

ADD TRANSITIONS ➤ *p. 194*

1. Switch to Slide Sorter view.
2. Select the slide that you want to transition *from* (or pick the first slide if you want to transition *into* your presentation).
3. Pick a transition effect from the drop-down list.

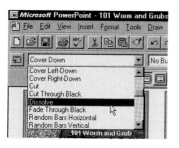

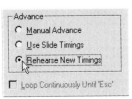

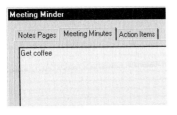

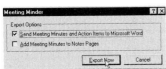

ADD BUILDS ➤ pp. 195-196

1. Click on the slide of interest in Slide Sorter view.
2. Choose a build effect from the Text Build Effects list.
3. Switch to the Slide Show view to see the build effect.

REHEARSE AND FINE-TUNE PRESENTATION TIMING ➤ pp. 197-199

1. Choose View|Slide Show.
2. Pick Rehearse New Times from the Advance options.
3. Click the Show button. A little clock/button appears in the lower-left corner of the screen.
4. When the current slide's been onscreen long enough to present the topic, click the clock/button to advance to the next slide.
5. Continue this way through the entire show. At the end of the show, PowerPoint will tell you the total running time, and ask if you want to record the timings. Click Yes or No.
6. Switch to Slide Sorter view, to see the rehearsal times. (You can change individual times.)

TAKE NOTES WHILE PRESENTING ➤ pp. 201-202

1. During the slide show, right-click anywhere on the screen.
2. Choose Meeting Minder from the shortcut menu.
3. Click the desired tab and type your note.
4. Click OK to dismiss the Meeting Minder.

EXPORT MEETING NOTES TO MICROSOFT WORD ➤ pp. 202-203

1. Open the Meeting Minder using the shortcut menu.
2. Click Export.
3. Choose the Export option.
4. Click Export Now.

PRINT MEETING NOTES ➤ pp. 204-205

Export meeting notes prior to printing. Use Microsoft Word's Print command to print notes exported to Word. For notes added to slides, visit the PowerPoint Print dialog box and choose Notes Pages from the Print what list.

It's almost showtime. Palms sweating, mind abuzz. Have you done your homework? This chapter contains dozens of tips to make your presentation a hit. Even if you *always* use 35mm slides or overhead transparencies, and never do onscreen presentations to audiences, you'll want to read this chapter, since you can use your computer's monitor for rehearsing.

We'll start by looking at the steps to present a manually controlled onscreen slide show. Then we will move to the topics of transitions and builds—ways to make your presentations more visually interesting. Next, we'll look at automatically advancing slides, and some helpful rehearsal tools. Finally, we'll explore the Meeting Minder, a handy note-taking and exporting facility to be used when presenting.

HARDWARE CONSIDERATIONS

Unless you have a monster monitor on your computer, desktop slide shows are best for rehearsing and for very small group huddles. For medium-sized groups, or for convention booths and the like, consider using larger projection TVs or professional video projectors and screens. These can be rented through many audio-visual rental houses. (Genigraphics also rents them, and will ship most anywhere. See Chapter 10 for information about Genigraphics.) Hotels and convention centers can also provide them. They are not cheap, and you will probably need an adapter box to convert your computer's video output as well as the proper cabling between the projection device and your computer, so be sure you rent from someone knowledgeable; and try to plug it all together a day or two early.

A RANT ...

Why can't we give a presentation without some kind of audio-visual equipment meltdown? You've seen it. Rhodes scholars, Nobel laureates, doctors, lawyers—all looking like idiots because their slide show's screwed up.

Chances are they all have one thing in common. They didn't rehearse with their final material in the room where the presentation was to be given on the equipment that was to be used for the real show (preferably on the *day of the show*).

I know, you are busy, and can't always do that. But whenever possible, TRY. As I've mentioned repeatedly, some projectors don't throw certain colors very well. If you are using someone else's computer for an electronic presentation, does it have enough RAM for that beefy slide number 12 with the full-color photo, or will it freeze? Does the borrowed or rented computer have the proper fonts, or are you headed for disaster? The *only* way to minimize embarrassment is rehearsal. There. That's off my chest.

SHOWTIME!

When opening a slide show with the Open command, PowerPoint will open in the Slide Sorter view. The last slide you were working with will be selected. So, after opening the presentation file, it is a good idea to switch to your first slide unless you want to start at some other point in the presentation. Remember, the selected slide will be the first one displayed when you switch to Slide Show view.

The easiest way to move to the first slide regardless of the view you are in is to press the HOME key on your keyboard. Other methods vary with the view you are using:

- In *Slide Sorter view*, click on the first slide.
- In *Outline view*, click on the first slide's icon.
- In *Slide view*, drag the scroll box at the left of your screen all the way to the top. Watch the slide numbers that appear as you drag.

Begin the slide show either by picking Slide Show from the View menu or clicking on the Slide Show button at the bottom-left of your screen. (The button looks like a projection screen on a stand.) All of PowerPoint's familiar menus and other tools will disappear.

CAUTION

If you switch to Slide Show view with a hidden slide selected, the hidden slide will be displayed immediately.

upgrade note

The Office Toolbar now automatically hides itself for slide shows.

In the bottom-left corner of the slide show screen you'll see a new, fairly large button used to access a pop-up menu.

If you are displaying a complex background, the button blends in, and might be difficult to see, so you will need to look for the button's telltale shadows and highlights. I've illustrated in black and white here so that it is easier to see.

Clicking the button or simply right-clicking anywhere on the screen reveals a shortcut menu like this one:

SHORTCUT

Right-click anywhere on the screen to reveal the shortcut menu instead of fumbling around for the onscreen button.

Now you have a piece of electronic "chalk" which you can turn on and off and use to scribble temporary onscreen lines while presenting:

Notice that in the Slide Show dialog box, you can control the color of the pen. This is very useful if you know you'll be highlighting things that have a light background, for instance, because you'll want to use a dark pen.

You can erase anything you've written by pressing E. Also, you might find it easier to write from top to bottom; you'd probably do this anyway, but it's worth mentioning.

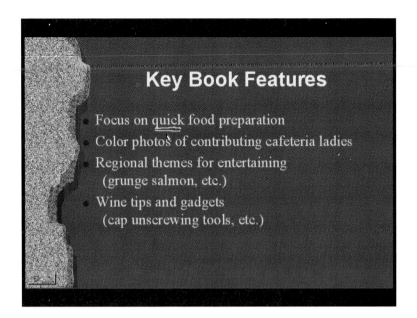

To enable the pen, either click on the button in the lower-left corner of your screen, or right-click, then choose Pen from the shortcut menu. To draw, just use your mouse and mouse buttons.

The scribbles do not permanently scar your masterpieces. Press the E key on your keyboard to erase all onscreen marks. And, when you switch to another slide, the drawings will vanish. That's the good news and the bad news. If someone "chalks" something important, *make notes*, because the electronic chalk marks will be squirted like watermelon seeds out of the universe when you change slides. Chalk it up to experience.

Pointing with Your Mouse

You can use your mouse pointer while presenting. Move it around the screen to point to things you wish to emphasize. To hide or redisplay the mouse pointer (and the little drawing button) press A or = (the equal sign).

CAUTION

Some slides may take a while to load and display. Be patient. Don't keep clicking the mouse or mashing a keyboard key. This will not speed things up. Worse, it might advance you past your target slide.

definition

Drill down: *To switch to original source material in a PowerPoint presentation. For example, to view an Excel worksheet that was the source of numbers used on a slide. (Practice before trying this in front of an audience!)*

Manually Advancing Slides

To manually move from slide to slide, you can do any of the following:

- To advance to the next slide, press the SPACEBAR, click the primary (usually the left) mouse button, or press N, RIGHT ARROW, DOWN ARROW, or PAGE DOWN.
- To go back one slide, press the BACKSPACE key, click the non-primary (usually the right) mouse button, or press P, LEFT ARROW, UP ARROW, or PAGE UP.
- To go to a specific slide, type the slide number, and press ENTER. For example, to go to slide 5, you'd type **5** and then hit ENTER.
- To quit a slide show and return to the previous view press ESC, or CTRL-BREAK, or either of your computer's minus keys.

VIEWING SLIDES OUT OF ORDER

From time to time you may need to present slides out of sequence ("branch," in PowerPoint parlance) in response to questions from your audience or to reiterate a detail. PowerPoint makes this easy to accomplish.

Branching and "Drilling Down"

During your presentation you can branch to a slide out of sequence whenever the need arises by simply typing the slide number and pressing ENTER. Alternately, you can right-click and choose Go from the menu. You can also "drill down" to reach the source of the information on the current slide if you've included linked, embedded objects.

Simply double-click on embedded or linked objects to bring up the source document. Alternately, you can use the Drilling Down button on the Standard toolbar. (This assumes, of course, that the source docu-

CAUTION

When you display the Slide Navigator, it lists the titles of hidden slides (discussed in a moment). If you don't want to tip your hand, don't use the Slide Navigator in front of your audience, unless you use really obtuse titles for hidden slides.

ment is on the computer being used for the presentation.) Realize too that the process can sometimes be painfully slow. So rehearse first if you plan to show off this way in a big meeting.

The Slide Navigator

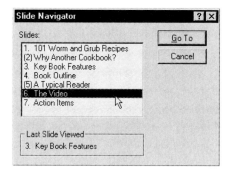

The Slide Navigator displays a list of slides and their titles. This is handy if you don't remember the number of a particular slide. To reach the Slide Navigator while presenting:

1. Click the right (non-primary) mouse button.
2. Choose Go To from the shortcut menu.
3. Choose Slide Navigator from the resulting submenu.
4. Scroll if necessary to select the desired slide.
5. Double-click its title to display the slide and dismiss the dialog box.
6. Remember that if the slide has builds, you'll need to advance the slides normally after reaching the first image to see all of the information. (Builds are discussed later in this chapter.)

HIDING AND REVEALING SLIDES

Slides can be included in your presentation file but hidden so they do not automatically show in the presentation. For instance, you might be presenting to a group of employees, and not want to discuss pending layoffs unless the topic raises its ugly head from the audience. Or you might want to have alternative pricing plans for customers in case the body language turns stiff when they see your opening numbers. The best way to prepare for these eventualities is to create multiple slides for the given topic and hide the ones you hope not to use.

Hiding Slides

Obviously, you need to do this *before* presenting:

1. Switch to Slide Sorter view.
2. Select the slide or slides you wish to hide (remember you can SHIFT-click).
3. Click the Hide Slide button.
4. The slide number or numbers will be covered with gray boxes and a diagonal slash.

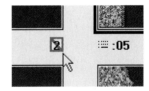

Displaying Hidden Slides

You can display a hidden slide at any time by typing its number and pressing ENTER. Pressing H will also reveal a hidden slide, but you must press H while viewing the slide *preceding* the hidden one.

Alternatively, you can use the Slide Navigator to display hidden slides. This was discussed earlier in this chapter.

Hiding Slides with White or Black Screens

If a slide is distracting your audience and you want to temporarily hide it without advancing to the next slide, press B to blacken the screen or W to make the screen all white. These choices toggle, so pressing B when the screen is black or W when the screen is white will bring your slide back into view.

CAUTION

Hidden slides don't get displayed in your shows unless you force them, but slide numbers don't change. Savvy audience members may notice that your onscreen numbers jump from, let's say, 10 to 12 and they may challenge you. Be ready to explain. Or, just don't number your slides!

TRANSITION AND BUILD EFFECTS

You know those fancy video transition effects weather forecasters use on the television news? Some remind you of venetian blinds, others look like confetti. Or a nearly blank slide fades up, then lines of text reveal themselves one at a time to *build* the completed slide. PowerPoint provides its own suite of transition and build effects which you can add to your onscreen shows. Here's how.

Adding Transitions

Transition effects dictate how one slide leaves the screen and how the next arrives.

1. Switch to Slide Sorter view.
2. Select the slide that you want to transition *from* (or pick the first slide if you want to transition *into* your presentation).
3. Pick a transition effect from the drop-down list.

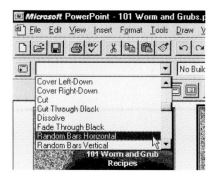

4. Watch the *selected slide* in Slide Sorter view as you pick the effect. It will demonstrate the transition for you.
5. Select the next slide and choose another effect.
6. You may need to switch to Slide Show to understand the full impact of these transitions, then switch back to Slide Sorter and try other effects until you see one you like. Some combinations work well together on adjacent slides, like Cover Right and Uncover Left. Experiment.

SHORTCUT

You can select multiple slides and apply the same effect to all of them at once. Simply hold down the SHIFT key while you click on each of the slides you wish to influence.

SHORTCUT

If you don't like any of the sounds that come with PowerPoint, you can use ones that you've created. Just choose Other from the Sound list to reach a standard Windows Open dialog box and round up the usual suspects.

Removing Transitions

To remove transitions, select the slide or slides of interest and choose No Transition from the transition list.

Changing the Speed of Transitions

To change the speed of transitions, use the Slide Transition button (next to the transition list) to reveal the Slide Transition dialog box. The preview box shows you what the transition will look like. As you can see here, I caught one mid-transition!

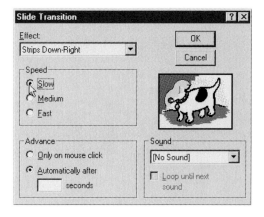

Pick Slow, Medium, or Fast from the Speed section. Faster is usually better.

Playing Sounds During Transitions

Another neat trick is to add sound to the transition. (Assuming, of course, that machines used to create and show the presentation all have audio capabilities.) You can choose among a number of sounds from the Sound list. Want applause? A camera click? Breaking glass? An explosion? Any of these is only a mouse click away.

Builds

Don't you hate it when you project a slide, and half the room reads ahead and then interrupts with questions on topics you were going to cover in a moment anyway? Adding Builds can help you avoid this.

The quickest way to specify builds is to select the material that you wish to reveal in a series of steps, then click the Build button. It's located on the Slide Sorter toolbar.

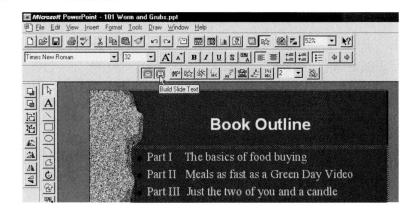

If you wish to add different effects to each individual object in the box, see the section "Using Other Animation Special Effects" later in this chapter.

For example, suppose you wanted to reveal a list of book sections one at a time.

1. Click on the slide of interest in Slide Sorter View.
2. Choose a build effect from the Text Build Effects list.
3. Switch to the Slide Show to see the build effect.

Each time you advance one "slide" (by clicking, pressing the SPACEBAR, etc.), the screen will reveal an additional bulletted line, until the entire build is complete.

Getting Film and Paper Copies of Build Slides

When you print handouts or export slides for film output, you'll be asked if you want to create an individual image for each build item or a single slide showing all of the elements. Pick the appropriate option for your situation.

habits & strategies

You can save paper and copying costs by not printing builds.

AUTOMATICALLY ADVANCING SLIDES

While most speakers like to manually advance slides in order to maintain full control over their presentations, you can ask PowerPoint

*If you forget the keyboard
controls while presenting in
Slide Show mode, press F1 for an
onscreen list of shortcuts. Don't
be embarrassed. Remember:
Nobody else in the room can run
AV equipment either. Click OK or
press ENTER to make the help
screen disappear.*

to change slides at timed intervals. This works well for trade shows where you want to let a presentation run continuously and unattended, or when you have a precise presentation time limit that you cannot exceed.

Even when you let PowerPoint advance slides at timed intervals, you can intervene. Here's how automatic advancing is accomplished:

1. Open your presentation in Slide Sorter view.
2. Click or SHIFT-click to select the slide or slides for which you plan to specify an onscreen time.
3. Click on the Slide Transition button to reveal the Slide Transition dialog box illustrated a moment ago.
4. Click in the box next to the word Seconds and enter the desired onscreen time. (The Automatically After button will be automatically selected for you.)
5. Pick a transition effect while in this dialog box, if you haven't already.
6. Click OK.
7. To rehearse, choose View|Slide Show|Select the Use Slide Timings, then click Show, and see how the timings feel to you. Remember you can always use the keyboard and mouse buttons to advance or go back.
8. There's another keyboard trick worth knowing: To pause the automatic advance feature, press the s key.

REHEARSING AND CHANGING SLIDE TIMING

After you've rehearsed or presented a show a few times, you may decide to "tweak" slide timing. In fact, PowerPoint can "watch" you give the show and "learn" the timings. (Just don't stop to answer the phone while doing this.)

1. Choose Slide Show from the View menu.
2. Pick Rehearse New Times from the Advance options.
3. Click the Show button. A little clock/button appears in the lower-left screen corner.

4. When the current slide's been onscreen long enough, click the clock/button to advance to the next.

5. Continue this way through the entire show. At the end of the show, PowerPoint will tell you the total running time, and ask if you want to record the timings (then choose Yes or No).

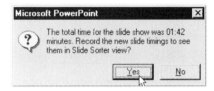

6. If you have recorded timings, you will see them listed under each slide. (You can change individual times here as well.)

Using the Slide Meter

PowerPoint's Slide Meter can watch you rehearse your presentation and tell you if you are manually advancing slides too fast or two slow in comparison to the times stored for each slide after your last successful rehearsal.

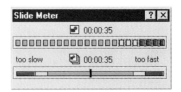

Here are the basic steps:

1. Rehearse and save the desired times (switch to Slide Sorter view if you like and change the times for any slides you like).
2. Start the slide show with Slide 1 (making sure to reset the Advance option to Manual Advance).
3. Right-click anywhere on the screen.
4. Choose Slide Meter.
5. A Slide Meter window appears with the "meter running."
6. Advance the slides manually.
7. Watch the position of the black vertical bar on the meter to see if you are going faster or slower than the saved slide times.

RUNNING A PRESENTATION CONTINUOUSLY

To run a presentation nonstop (in a trade show booth, for instance):

1. Open the presentation.
2. Make sure all your slides have transition times assigned to them.
3. Choose Slide Show from the View menu. You'll see the Slide Show dialog box.

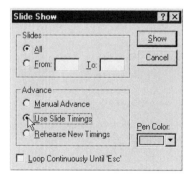

4. Select the range of slides to be shown (or use the All default).
5. Select Use Slide Timings in the Advance section of the Slide Show dialog box.

CAUTION

Don't (even though the Microsoft manual suggests this) unplug the keyboard and/or mouse with your computer running. You could damage your hardware.

6. Click the Loop Continuously until 'Esc' box.
7. Click the Show button.
8. The show will run continuously until you press the ESC key (but watch it in its entirety before going on that coffee break, just in case).
9. Move the keyboard and mouse out of sight and out of reach to frustrate the mischievous.

USING OTHER ANIMATION SPECIAL EFFECTS

PowerPoint now comes with a wonderful array of animation effects. You can make text pinwheel in, drive by, drop in, etc. I wish I could show you these effects, because they are incredibly cool. But books can't show motion. You apply these animation effects as follows:

1. In Slide Sorter view, find the slide to which you wish to apply effects.
2. Click the Animation Effects button on the Standard toolbar. This brings up the Animation Effects toolbar.
3. Click the objects you wish to emphasize.
4. Then click the appropriate button on the toolbar.

5. You can also choose an option from one of the Build Slide Text submenus found on the Tools menu. If you choose Build Slide Text and then Other, the Animation Effects dialog box appears.

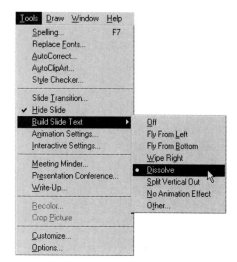

6. Here you can make all sorts of adjustments to how your animation works. You can even specify what should happen to items after the build (e.g., fade, become a certain color, etc.).

THE MEETING MINDER FOR NOTE-TAKING

The Meeting Minder lets you pop up a dialog box containing three tabs where you can make notes. After the meeting, you can add the notes to your presentation file or export them to a new Microsoft Word file.

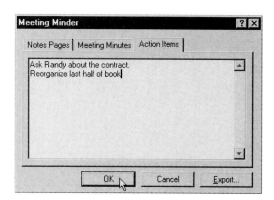

Taking Notes with Meeting Minder

1. Start the presentation.
2. Whenever you get to a point where you want to add a note, right-click anywhere on the screen.
3. Choose Meeting Minder from the shortcut menu.
4. Click the desired tab (Notes Pages, Meeting Minutes, or Action Items).
5. Type and edit notes using the usual bag of Windows 95 text tricks.
6. Click OK to dismiss the Meeting Minder.
7. Repeat steps 2-6 until you are done with the meeting.

Exporting Meeting Minder Notes

Once you've completed your presentation you can export your notes either to a Microsoft Word document or to the slides themselves. It is even possible to automatically create a new Action Items slide.

- Items you type in the Notes or Meeting Minutes tabs can be exported to a Word document or added to PowerPoint slide notes.
- Items typed in the Action Items tab will automatically appear in a new "last slide" titled Action Items.

Exporting to Microsoft Word

To create a Word document from your Meeting Minder notes:

1. Choose Tools|Meeting Minder.
2. Click the Export button.
3. Select the Send Meeting Minutes and Action Items to Microsoft Word choice.
4. Click the Export Now button.
5. Word will launch if it isn't already running and PowerPoint will export the notes to a new Word document complete with slide titles and other helpful information.

6. Run Word's spelling checker. (We all make typos and misspellings in meetings.)

7. Save the Word file to preserve your notes.

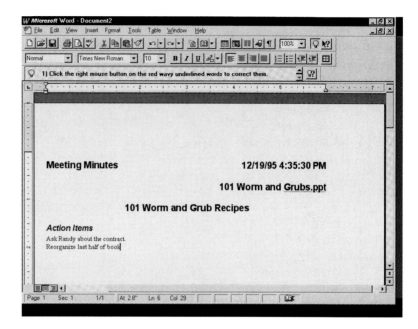

Exporting to PowerPoint Slide Notes

To move your Meeting Minder notes to the notes sections of slides:

1. In Slide Show view, right-click and choose Meeting Minder to open the Meeting Minder.

2. Click the Export button.

3. Select the Add Meeting Notes to Notes Pages choice.

4. PowerPoint will add the notes to the appropriate slides.

5. You might want to run both PowerPoint's spelling and style checkers before saving the PowerPoint presentation file.

6. Save your PowerPoint presentation to save the notes.

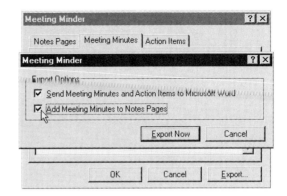

Exporting Action Items to an Action Items Slide

Anything you type in the Action Items tab of the Meeting Minder will appear in a new last slide called Action Items:

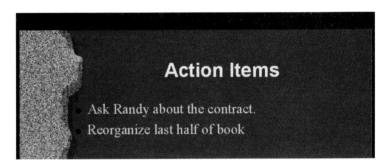

You might want to run PowerPoint's spelling checker before saving the PowerPoint presentation file (and therefore your new slide containing Action Items notes).

Printing Meeting Minder Notes

To print notes exported to Word, use Word's Print command or the little Print icon in Word's Standard toolbar.

To print notes saved in your PowerPoint presentation file:

1. Choose Print from PowerPoint's File menu.

2. Choose Note Pages from the Print What portion of the Print dialog box.
3. Change any other options as necessary (number of copies, etc.).
4. Click OK.

WHAT'S NEXT?

The end is nigh! If you never share presentation files with others you can skip Chapter 12. It's for folks who collaborate. Chapter 13 is for people who want to change the look and feel of PowerPoint—you know, mess with toolbars, change the startup sequence, things like that. You already know most of the good stuff. If I were you, I'd be tempted to try a presentation or two now and visit the last two chapters after I had a few dozen great-looking slides under my belt.

Sharing Presentation Files with Others

207

FAST FORWARD

COPY SLIDES FROM
OTHER PRESENTATIONS ➤ *pp. 210-211*

To copy and paste from one presentation to another or to insert entire presentations, choose the command Slides from File. It can be found on the Insert menu. In either case, slides take on the design elements of the destination presentation.

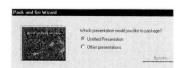

PACK AND GO ➤ *pp. 211-214*

1. Carefully check and polish your presentation. Keep it simple. Multimedia elements, fancy fonts, and the like increase the likelihood of frustration on the road.
2. Have plenty of floppies ready if that's the way you will transport your presentation.
3. Choose File|Pack and Go.
4. Answer the wizard's questions.
5. PowerPoint will pack (compress) the necessary files.
6. Try loading the compressed files on a different computer before you travel.

NETWORK CONFERENCE ➤ *pp. 217-218*

1. Open the presentation and choose Tools|Presentation Conference, then list the attendees' computer names.
2. Attendees open any PowerPoint presentation and also choose Presentation Conference from their Tools menus.
3. When all listed attendees are "present," you can run the show.
4. Participants watch, and can scribble on their screens for all to see.

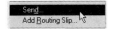

E-MAIL POWERPOINT
PRESENTATIONS ➤ *pp. 221-223*

If Microsoft Exchange is properly installed, the File menu should have the choices Send and Add Routing Slip, which can be used to send PowerPoint files via e-mail.

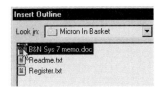

CONVERT MICROSOFT WORD FILES
TO POWERPOINT SHOWS ➤ *pp. 220-221*

1. Begin a new presentation or open an existing one.
2. Choose the Insert|Slides from Outline to insert the heading text from Microsoft Word files. (Each Heading 1 will start a new slide.)
3. Select the Word file containing the heading text, and click the Insert button.
4. Add other text, multimedia elements, etc.
5. Style and spell check.
6. Save your new PowerPoint presentation.

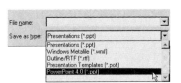

CONVERT TO AND FROM
DIFFERENT POWERPOINT VERSIONS ➤ *p. 223*

- PowerPoint version 7 (a.k.a. PowerPoint 95) will recognize, convert, and open presentations created with older PowerPoint versions.
- When you close converted presentations you will be asked if you want to save them as new version files. If you do, use a new file name to preserve the old version just in case.
- To use new (version 7) files with older PowerPoint versions, use the Save As command, and change the file type to the earlier version to create useable files. They might not have all the fancy animation and other new features, but they should be viewable.

You can share your presentations with other computer users in several ways. The most obvious is to play "pass the floppy" or to send a copy of the presentation file via network or modem. If you are on a network, you can "give" the presentation over the network while others watch on their computers. Participants in these networked PowerPoint conferences can even draw on their screens for the benefit of each other.

These straightforward approaches will work if other users have the same version of PowerPoint on their computers, or if you give them the PowerPoint Viewer along with any unusual fonts you've used in your presentation. We've got a lot of ground to cover. Let's dance.

COPYING SLIDES FROM OTHER PRESENTATIONS

Perhaps the lowest tech form of sharing is copying slides from one presentation to another. It's pretty simple, actually. You can work in any view you like, but I prefer Slide Sorter view, so that's what I will illustrate in this example. Here are the steps:

1. Open both presentations (in Slide Sorter view for this example).
2. Switch to the "source" presentation by visiting the Window menu.
3. Select and copy the slide or slides to be included. (Click or SHIFT-click, then choose Edit|Copy or use the CTRL-C shortcut.)
4. Switch to the destination presentation.
5. Position the insertion point by clicking between the two slides where the inserted slides will go.
6. Choose Edit|Paste or use the CTRL-V shortcut.

7. The slide or slides will be inserted and will take on the look of the destination template (design and color scheme, etc.). Even OLE links should work.

8. Examine the results, run the style checker, and save the newly improved presentation.

Inserting an Entire Presentation into Another

Use the Insert menu's Slides from File command to insert entire PowerPoint presentations into a destination presentation.

1. Open the destination presentation.
2. Switch to Slide Sorter view.
3. Click between the slides where you want the new slides to be inserted.
4. Choose Insert|Slides from File.
5. Locate the PowerPoint presentation to be inserted.
6. Click Insert.
7. The slides will be inserted and take on the design characteristics of the destination presentation. All the slides will be renumbered as necessary.

PACK AND GO WIZARD

In theory, the Pack and Go Wizard is your friend. It looks at your presentation, asks you a few questions, and with luck, puts a (compressed) copy of the presentation, along with any necessary sound, multimedia, and other files, on a disk or disks, which you can then take with you to load onto a different computer. Pack and go—get it? It works. At least sometimes. Before you see how, here are some general tips:

- Try using Pack and Go completely several times *before* the cab comes to take you to the airport. That is to say, pack your presentation on one computer and unpack it on another several times when you are not in a huge hurry. You see, Pack and Go is neither quick nor flawless.

- Pack and Go will only work if the machine you are visiting runs Windows 95 (as opposed to 3.1 or Windows for Workgroups or whatever).

CAUTION

You can not *undo the insertion of slides with the Insert Slides from File or Insert Slides from Outline command. Save your work just before using these commands, then check your updated presentation carefully before saving again. Quit without saving if things get too screwed up, then try again.*

CAUTION

The version of Pack and Go that comes with PowerPoint 95 will only work with other Windows 95 or Windows NT machines. If you plan to visit sites with earlier Windows versions or Macs, skip this topic and see "Working with Different Versions of PowerPoint," later in this chapter.

- It is best if the machine you are visiting has the latest version of PowerPoint, although you *can* take along something called the *PowerPoint Viewer* for stripped-down slide shows sans bells and whistles. (The Viewer and the process of converting PowerPoint presentations to earlier versions are both described later in this chapter.)
- If possible, send ahead a "packed" copy of your presentation so that it can be unpacked and tested at the other end before you arrive. (I know, I know ... so at least send a draft.)
- Travel light. *Simple is better when you pack and go.* Every sound, and video, and OLE link, and other gimmick you pack is a potential landmine.
- Stick with standard Windows 95 fonts if you can.

Packing

Keeping the tips I've just listed firmly in mind, follow these steps for packing if you plan to visit someone else with a Windows 95 machine:

1. Check and double-check your presentation. Have your pickiest coworker proof it too. You *don't* want to pack over and over, trust me.
2. Prepare or locate some blank floppies, if that's how you plan to carry around your presentation. (You can use other media, including those nifty ZIP removable disk drives if the destination computer will support it.)
3. Choose File|Pack and Go.
4. You will see a wizard. Read each dialog box and make the necessary choices, which will vary with your situation. For example, you can choose floppies or a different media type.

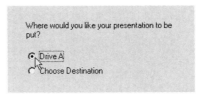

habits & strategies

Pack and Go and the PowerPoint Viewer don't seem to know about Windows 95's long filenames. So, when naming PowerPoint presentations you plan to take on the road, keep that in mind and use short, simple filenames containing no more than eight characters.

5. Feed floppies when asked, and *label* and *sequentially number* the floppies as they are removed!

6. If the Wizard is having trouble locating presentation elements—sound files, videos, etc.—you will be asked to locate them. The fuse is lit. (Repeat after me: "Simple is better. Simple is better.")

7. If there are links in your presentation, you should choose to include the links, but you will probably not be able to edit or drill down to links when you travel, unless the machine you are visiting has network access to the linked files. Even then—well ... simple is better. Got it? The fuse is getting shorter.

8. If you are using non-Windows 95 fonts, and if they are TrueType, and if they are embeddable, and if you don't mind carrying around lots of disks, you can take the fonts with you, but as you know, simple is better.

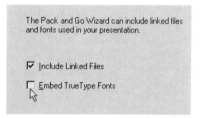

9. If the machine you are carrying the presentation to has the latest version of PowerPoint, you won't need to take the PowerPoint Viewer, so you can refuse to pack it when asked. (The PowerPoint Viewer is discussed later in this chapter.)

10. When you get to the Finish wizard screen you will be asked to feed floppies (if that's the chosen media). Click OK or press ENTER each time you flop swap.

11. If possible, test by unpacking on a different machine while you are still at home. (And don't say I didn't warn you.)

12. Pack the floppies carefully away from magnets (and consider making backup copies to carry with you in case the baggage handlers are having a bad day).

13. Got your tickets? Bon voyage! Knock 'em dead.

Unpacking

The files on the floppies (or other media) created by Pack and Go are useless as is. They need to be unpacked first. Here are the general steps, unpacking gods willing:

1. Place the first floppy in the drive. (This stranger's machine *does* have the right size drive, doesn't it?)
2. Double-click the My Computer icon (even though this probably isn't *your* computer).

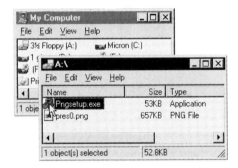

3. Double-click the appropriate floppy disk icon.
4. Double-click the Pngsetup.exe icon (that's Pack and Go setup in MS-DOS speak).
5. When asked, either type the name and location of the folder you wish to use to hold the presentation on the new machine, or better yet, type a new folder name and the setup utility will create it:

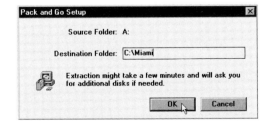

6. Write down the folder name and its location. Remember, you are a stranger in a strange land. Next time you want to run the presentation, you'll need to recall where you put your files, Gulliver.

7. Click OK, cross your fingers, and chant "There's no place like home. There's ..."

8. Soon you will get either really good or really bad news. If it's good, you will be given a chance to preview your unpacked presentation. I'd do that if I were you. If it's bad news, I don' know what to tell you. Try again, maybe with your backup disks.

Running Presentations After Unpacking

Immediately after unpacking, you'll be asked if you want to run the presentation. If the computer has the most recent version of PowerPoint installed, chances are when you say Yes, PowerPoint will launch and you can take the usual steps to show your slides. If PowerPoint is not installed, or if you are having a strange day, you might see the presentation running in the PowerPoint Viewer.

THE POWERPOINT VIEWER

The PowerPoint Viewer is a stripped-down version of PowerPoint that basically lets you flip through slides and write on them with the chalk thingie. Some of your animation effects might not work. There is no Meeting Minder, no shortcut menu, etc. That's why it is a good idea to rehearse every presentation you plan to use with the Viewer so that the nasty surprises occur in private (or at least in friendly territory).

You can give complete strangers copies of the PowerPoint Viewer. It's even okay with Microsoft. They said so! When you use Pack and Go, you are given a chance to pack a copy of the Viewer. (You need not use Pack and Go to pass around copies of the Viewer. Its name is Pptview.exe, by the way.)

To use the Viewer, open the folder containing it and double-click the Viewer's icon:

habits & strategies

If you can't find the PowerPoint Viewer file (Pptview.exe), use Windows 95's Find feature. It is described in Appendix A.

You will be asked to locate the presentation that you hope to display. (All those nice long Windows 95 filenames will look like guacamole, but don't panic. You'll figure it out.) Double-click the presentation du jour, as shown in Figure 12.1.

The presentation will launch, and you will see the first slide. Things like sound and multimedia objects should work as long as the stranger's machine has the right hardware and supporting software (a sound card and speakers, a QuickTime viewer for QuickTime movies, etc.). Simple. Think simple.

Use the SPACEBAR or RIGHT ARROW key to advance slides and the LEFT ARROW key to go back. Hidden slides remain hidden unless you

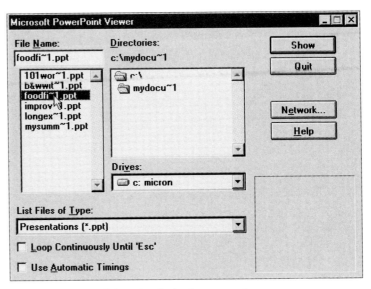

Figure 12.1 Double-click on the desired presentation.

press the H key to advance. Press ESC to end the presentation. The B and W keys work to blank the screen. Remember? They toggle black or white screens.

That's about it where the viewer is concerned. It *is* possible to create a *play list* so that the Viewer can show multiple presentations in sequence, but I'll let you explore online Help or the bigger books if that feature intrigues you.

PRESENTATION CONFERENCING AND NETWORKING

Okay, you people who hate meeting face-to-face, this one's for you. It is possible (notice I said *possible*, not *easy*) to sit at your desk and run a PowerPoint presentation while others on your network watch it on their computer screens. They can even scribble on their screens to everyone's enjoyment and frustration. Of course, unless you have a really loud voice, or know how to conference call, or have some fancy, networkable audio-broadcasting software, participants won't be able to hear you (or each other), but hey. And did I mention that everybody needs to have legal copies of the current version of PowerPoint? Here are the general steps.

Finding Audience Members' Computer Names or Numbers

You need to know the name of each audience member's computer. Here are the general steps for learning the names:

1. Choose Settings from the Windows 95 Start menu.
2. Pick Control Panel from the resulting submenu.
3. Double-click the network icon, as shown in Figure 12.2.
4. Click the Identification tab.
5. Read and write down the Computer name exactly as it appears on the screen.
6. Tell the presenter.

SHORTCUT

It is possible to save lists of audience members to save a lot of retyping. Ask your network folks for help with this.

CAUTION

There is a known problem with some versions of Novell's IP software and PowerPoint's conferencing toys. Disabling Novell's IP drivers and using the TCP/IP implementation that comes with Windows 95 should help. Ask your network guru for technical assistance if you are having trouble here.

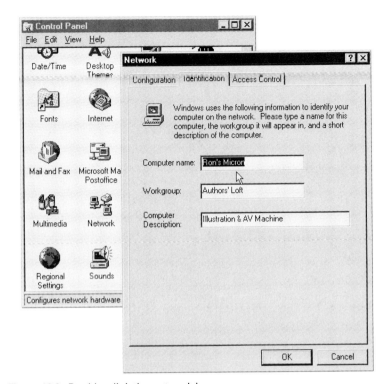

Figure 12.2 Double-click the network icon.

Setting up to Present

If you are the presenter, you have some additional work to do before things can get under way.

1. Fire up the PowerPoint presentation of the day and choose Presentation Conference from the Tools menu.
2. Click the Presenter button in the resulting wizard and then click Next or press ENTER.
3. Pick the desired "Stage Manager" options (Meeting Minder, Slide Navigator, and/or Slide Meter) and move ahead one step.
4. Type the exact names of the networked computers to be used by each audience member. (You will also almost certainly need help from your network guru since this feature has a hard time locating participants even when you

CAUTION

If your name is on the audience list, you'd darn well better be present and accounted for at show time. It cannot start without you. Let the presenter know if that's a problem so that your name can be removed from the audience list.

name them properly. While you are at it, have your network administrator set up lists of audience members to minimize future delays.)

5. Once everyone in your audience list has logged on (see below) you can present pretty much as if you were standing at a podium. If you are using Meeting Minder, Slide Navigator, etc., you will see these tools on your screen, but other participants will not see them on their screens. If you draw or point with your mouse, they will see that, however.

Being an Audience Member

When the presentation is ready, the presenter tells you (telepathically, or via e-mail, perhaps) that the time has come.

1. Each audience member on the list needs to open a presentation and choose Tools|Presentation Conference.
2. Y'all must choose to be members of the audience when the wizard asks:

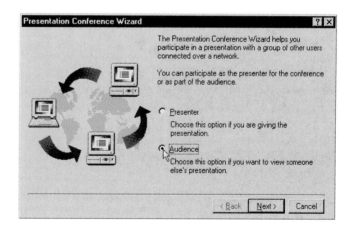

3. The show will not start until *everyone* is logged on (but you need not be seated or paying attention).
4. Audience members can sit back and relax. Mumble under your breath. Eat a bagel. Draw if you like, but don't get obscene. Others can see what you scribble on your screen.

CONVERTING WORD AND OTHER DOCUMENTS TO PRESENTATIONS

You might be able to save some typing by inserting text directly from Microsoft Word and other programs. One way is to simply open both programs and copy things from the other program and paste them into PowerPoint slides. Frequently, a better way is to use PowerPoint's inserting (importing) capabilities. Here are the general steps for importing headings from a Microsoft Word file:

1. Inspect, and possibly reformat, the Microsoft Word or other document containing the text you want to import, as shown in Figure 12.3. (For example, in Word, only text formatted as Headings will be imported.)
2. Save the Word or other program file and close it.
3. Open an existing PowerPoint presentation or begin a new one (pick a pleasing design if starting a new one).

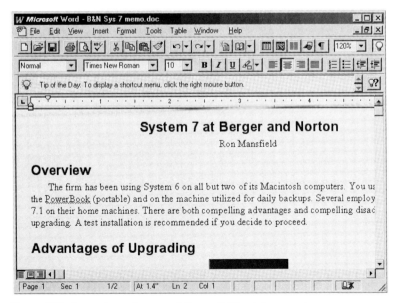

Figure 12.3 Preparing to import a Microsoft Word document.

4. Switch to Outline or Slide Sorter view if you like, but that's not necessary.
5. If there are already slides in the destination presentation, select the slide just before where you want to insert the incoming text.
6. Choose Insert|Slides from File.
7. Locate the Word (or other) document containing the text of interest.

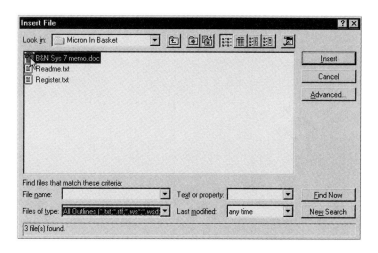

8. Hold your breath while PowerPoint imports. With luck, you'll have a new slide for each Heading 1 or equivalent. Heading levels 2 and lower will take their proper place, as shown in Figure 12.4.
9. Clean up the text, run the style and spell checkers, and generally treat the text like any other.

PowerPoint can also import raw text files, RTF files, WordStar files, Works files, Excel worksheets, WordPerfect files, and more. Experiment.

MAILING AND ROUTING PRESENTATIONS

If you have Microsoft Exchange installed on your networked computer, you can send PowerPoint files along with notes via e-mail, as shown in Figure 12.5. Use the Send command on the File menu.

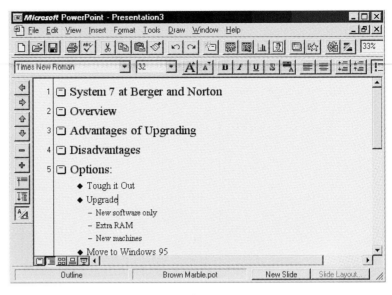

Figure 12.4 New slides from a Word document.

Instead of sending multiple copies to coworkers on your network, you can route one copy to multiple users. Use the Add Routing slip

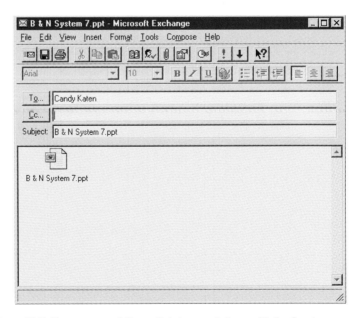

Figure 12.5 You can e-mail PowerPoint presentations with the Send command.

CAUTION

Never convert your only copy of a file to a new version. Always work with copies of files when fooling with document converters of any species!

command (also on the File menu) to do this. See your documentation for Exchange or another e-mail product to learn more.

WORKING WITH DIFFERENT VERSIONS OF POWERPOINT

It is possible to import PowerPoint files created with earlier versions (even files created on a Macintosh) and then save them as PowerPoint version 7 files. Simply open the documents and watch PowerPoint convert them before they are displayed. When you close an old file, PowerPoint will ask if you want to convert it.

It is also possible to save a brand spanking new PowerPoint version 7 file as, let's say, a PowerPoint version 4 file. In the process, you will lose spiffy new animation features and such, but hey, you can't have everything.

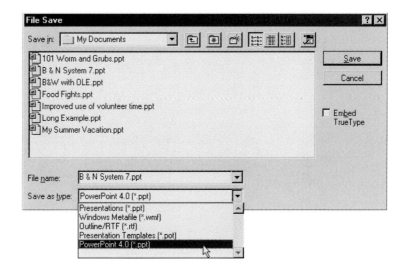

Be sure you use a different file name when saving as older versions, so that you will have both versions available.

A WORD ABOUT FONTS

If you've used only TrueType fonts in your presentation and think the recipient might not have the fonts, you can send them along with

habits & strategies

When sharing presentations with others on a network, it is sometimes possible to share "downloadable" fonts stored on the server. Check with your network administrator or help desk for assistance.

your presentation by clicking the Embed TrueType Fonts option in the Save As dialog box.

Sending along embedded fonts can greatly increase the size of a presentation file, so do it only when necessary. Not all TrueType fonts can be embedded this way. Experiment.

Obviously, if you plan to exchange presentations on floppy disks, file sizes should not exceed disk capacity, or you'll need to use some file compression or backup-and-restore scheme. For instance, most of the sample presentations in this book would be too big for most floppy formats.

Sharing Presentations with Macintosh Users

If you convert a presentation from Apple Macintosh to Microsoft Windows, you will probably not have the same fonts on both computers. You can replace fonts that you don't have with fonts you do have using the Replace Fonts command described in Chapter 5. Do you remember it?

1. Choose Replace Fonts on the Tools menu.
2. In the Replace box, click the font you want to change.
3. In the With box, click the font you want to substitute.

habits & strategies

Users without PowerPoint on their computers can play presentations (but not edit them) with the Viewer. You'll need one 1.44MB floppy for the Viewer and its installer, and another disk or disks for your presentation. Or you can pack the Viewer when using Pack and Go. See online Help.

Here are the fonts Microsoft recommends for replacement:

Macintosh Font	Windows Font
Avant Garde	Century Gothic
Bookman	Bookman Old Style
Helvetica	Arial
N Helvetica Narrow	Arial Narrow
New Century Schlbk	Century Schoolbook
Palatino	Book Antiqua
Times	Times New Roman
Zapf Chancery	Monotype Corsiva
Zapf Dingbats	Monotype Sorts

WHAT'S NEXT?

The bitter end, that's what's next. In Chapter 13 you'll learn how to personalize PowerPoint. Then school is out!

MEETING
IN
PROGRESS

FAX

Personalizing PowerPoint

INCLUDES

- Controlling what happens when you start PowerPoint

- Changing PowerPoint options

- Customizing toolbars

- Using custom spelling dictionaries

FAST FORWARD

CHANGE POWERPOINT OPTIONS ➤ pp. 230-237

1. Choose Options from the Tools menu.
2. Click the desired tab to reveal your options.
3. Click to add or remove check marks and make other changes.
4. Use the What's This? button to learn more about options.
5. Click OK when finished.
6. Quitting PowerPoint saves the changes.

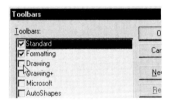

HIDE TOOLBARS ➤ p. 237

1. Right-click on a toolbar.
2. The shortcut menu will appear.
3. Click to remove the check mark from the toolbar you
   wish to hide.

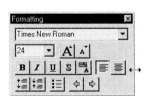

DISPLAY TOOLBARS ➤ pp. 237-238

1. Right-click on a toolbar or choose Toolbars from the
   View menu.
2. A list of available toolbars will appear.
3. Click to add a check mark next to the toolbar you wish
   to display.
4. Click OK if working in the Toolbars dialog box, or repeat
   steps 1 through 3 as necessary if using the shortcut menu
   method.

MOVE AND RESHAPE TOOLBARS ➤ p. 238

1. Point to any non-button portion of a toolbar and hold down
   the left mouse button.
2. The entire toolbar will be surrounded by a distinctive outline.
3. Drag. The outline will change shape and location as you drag.
4. The toolbar can "float" anywhere on your screen or be
   "docked" at any edge.

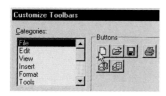

CUSTOMIZE TOOLBARS ➤ *pp. 238-240*

1. Make sure the toolbar you wish to modify is visible.
2. Choose Customize from the Tools menu.
3. Click a category to see the available toolbar buttons. (There is one for each PowerPoint command.)
4. Drag the button of interest to the desired toolbar.
5. When you release the mouse button, the new toolbar button will be inserted.
6. To remove a button, follow steps 1 through 3, then drag the button from the toolbar to anyplace else on your screen.

USE CUSTOM SPELLING DICTIONARIES ➤ *p. 240*

1. Make sure that the custom dictionary of your choosing is in the PROOF folder located in the MSAPPS folder, found in the Windows folder (**C:\WINDOWS\MSAPPS\PROOF**).
2. Choose Spelling from the Tools menu or use the Spelling button on the Standard toolbar.
3. Choose the desired dictionary from the drop-down list.
4. Click the Close button.

Microsoft's PowerPoint team spent a long time designing the "look and feel" of their baby. For many users, it's just fine the way it is. But having been in some software design meetings myself, I can tell you that there are often heated arguments about the demeanor of specific software features. And, while users like you and I are not as finicky as programmers, occasionally we find ourselves at odds about how a feature should work. Sometimes the only civilized solution to these spats is to create ways for users to personalize software settings.

PowerPoint permits this—perhaps not to the almost absurd extent that Microsoft Word users can fiddle, but you have plenty of control. For example, you can move and modify toolbars, control how text-editing features behave, and more. Let's take a look.

OPTIONS

Perhaps the widest variety of changes can be made using the Options choice on PowerPoint's Tools menu. It reveals the following dialog box. (Incidentally, you will need to have a presentation open to see the Tools menu.)

CAUTION

The techniques described in this chapter can affect the reliability of PowerPoint (particularly by playing havoc with wizards and certain Help features that "demonstrate" tasks). Moreover, your organization might prohibit customizing software, especially if you share your computer with coworkers. So, when in doubt, don't.

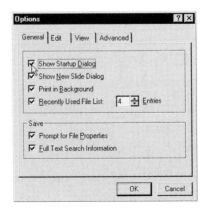

You can flit from tab to tab in this Swiss Army knife of a dialog box. Let's visit all the tabs, what say?

General Options Tab

The General tab cover reminds me of my hall closet. It contains a little bit of everything in no apparent order. This tab was probably designed on a late Sunday night near the programmers' deadline. Lemmie see, here...

Show Startup Dialog

You know the dialog that you see after the Tip of the Day? It looks like this:

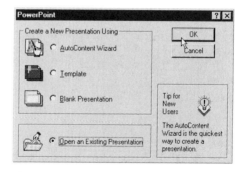

Removing the check (it is on by default) from the General tab's Show Startup Dialog checkbox bypasses that greeting, starts a new untitled presentation, and takes you directly to the New Slide dialog box. Speaking of which...

Show New Slide Dialog

Removing the default check mark from the Show New Slide option causes PowerPoint to launch with a new untitled presentation and display a blank title slide. Moreover, with the check mark removed from the Show New Slide checkbox, you won't see that handy New Slide dialog box each time you click the New Slide button. As nice as it is to start a new presentation by staring at the blank title slide, I miss the

habits & strategies

To avoid seeing tips of the day, remove the check mark from the Show Tips at Startup box in the Tip window.

Background Printing: *The Background Printing feature sends your presentation to a temporary disk file, and then from the disk to your printer, theoretically enabling you to do other work while Windows 95 "steals" time from the computer when it is not busy obeying your keyboard and mouse activities.*

New Slide dialog thereafter, and so I leave the Show New Slide Dialog feature on like PowerPoint's creators intended.

Print in Background

The Print in Background choice lets you work on other things while your PowerPoint presentation is printed. (Background printing is on by default.)

If you are very short on disk space, or if you are having trouble with printing, or if you want to speed up the overall printing process and do not need to do other work while waiting for the printer, consider removing the check mark.

Recently Used File List

This is where you specify the number of recently used presentation files that will appear on the bottom of the File menu.

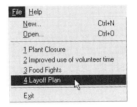

Removing the check mark prevents any files from showing up there, a good idea if you are working with presentations titled "Proposed Layoffs" or "Ways to Cut Corners in Our Employee Benefit Package," or whatever. Shame on you! By the way, the default is four filenames, the maximum is nine.

Prompt for File Properties

This choice causes the following intriguing Properties dialog box to appear whenever you save a file for the first time, or whenever you use the Save As command:

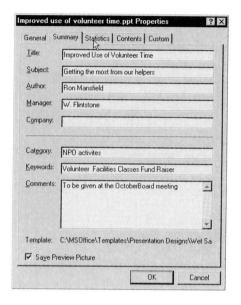

You can see a presentation's properties at any time by using the Properties command on the File menu.

Entering information into this dialog box makes it easier to find presentations based on keywords, author, and so on. It is also a good place to make notes to yourself or others about the presentation.

Full Text Search Option

The Full Text Search save option makes it easier for Windows 95 to help you find "lost" presentations based on the words within your presentation. The downside is this option makes presentation files slightly bigger.

Oh, yeah. The Full Text Search save option won't solve problems like finding text in drawings contained in your PowerPoint presentation. Better than a sharp stick in the eye, though.

Edit Options Tab

The Edit tab deals with text entry and appearance. All of the options are on by default. I personally leave all but one that way. I shut off Automatic Word Selection. Here's the scoop on all of the options.

Replace Straight Quotes with Smart Quotes

Smart Quotes converts those boring typewriter-style quotation marks (") with curvaceous typesetter's style quotes that seem to "hug" text. The only reason I can imagine you'd want to turn these off is if you plan to use quote marks for some non-standard purpose like drawing "ASCII art." As my tech editor pointed out, ASCII art is an oxymoron, isn't it?

Automatic Word Selection

Yuk. I hate it when I drag to select *part* of the word and the *whole damned thing* gets selected. There. I've said it. And thanks, Microsoft, for letting me turn off Automatic Word Selection.

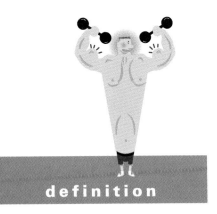

definition

Drag and Drop: A Microsoft feature found in many programs that lets you select text, then move or copy it with your mouse. Releasing the primary mouse button plunks the text in the position indicated by the mouse pointer. Drag... and drop... Get it?

Use Smart Cut and Paste

Smart Cut and Paste does a pretty good job of anticipating what you meant to do when you haphazardly cut and pasted (or dragged) sentences and their surrounding spaces. That is to say, it can often remove duplicate spaces and add missing spaces caused by cutting, pasting, and dragging. Ahh, computers.

Drag-and-Drop Text Editing

People normally either love or hate drag-and-drop text editing. Mostly I love it, although if I have to drag too far, I'll cut and paste instead. Anyhow. Leave it on and get in the habit of using it unless it drives you crazy.

Spelling Suggestions

The spelling checker does a pretty good job of guessing what your fat fingers and dull brain meant to type; then it offers a list of suggested alternate spellings. You can turn this off if you have a woefully slow machine and it annoys you. But then if things like this bother you, why are you using such an old machine? Fuel the nation's economy. Upgrade that hardware, please.

View Options Tab

The View options are pretty self-explanatory, and I know you are busy, and this is the end of the book, so I'll be brief. Here goes.

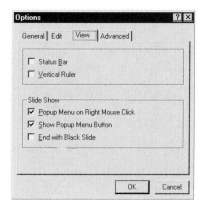

Status Bar

This option displays helpful comments at the bottom of your screen as you work. Who doesn't need help? Unless you have a tiny screen and a big project, leave this option enabled.

Vertical Ruler

This choice turns the vertical ruler on and off. I can't imagine the design team fight that prompted this option. Live a little. Leave it on.

Slide Show Options

Except for Show Popup Menu Button, the choices in the Slide Show section of the Options dialog box's View tab are easy to understand.

The Show Popup Menu Button choice displays or hides that little button when you do onscreen presentations:

Advanced Options Tab

You and I are almost done with this book now! Here's the last tab of the Options dialog box.

Maximum Number of Undos

This is where you proscribe the maximum number of Undo actions PowerPoint will remember and let you perform. The default is 20, which works for me; the maximum is 150.

24-Bit Graphics

Unless you have a really slow computer (display), enable the Render 24-bit Bitmaps at Highest Quality choice. Your onscreen graphics will look better.

Export Pictures

Use the two Export Pictures choices to improve either the printed or onscreen appearance of graphics. You can switch back and forth for

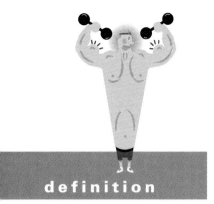

definition

Path: *A description of the location of a file including the disk drive's letter and the folder name(s) necessary to reach the file, separated by slashes; e.g., C:\MyDocuments\Presentations\ Board Meetings. See also 1970s technology.*

printing and screen-intensive tasks if you like. Experiment to see if this makes a noticeable difference on your system.

Default File Location

Unless you tell PowerPoint otherwise, it offers to store all of your new presentations in your My Documents folder. To change that default setting, you type (yes, I said "type") the path (yes, I said "path") in the long, white empty box. So, if you want to store your stuff in, say, the Exxon folder located in your Client folder on your D drive you would type **D:\CLIENT\EXXON.** Sorry, folks, no Browse button here to let you find the folder of your dreams.

TOOLBARS

You can fiddle with those handy toolbar buttons to your heart's content. You can hide toolbars, display them, change their contents, even create your own button faces. Here, look.

Display and Hide Toolbars

There are two handy ways to display additional toolbars. The first is quickest if there is already at least one toolbar on your screen. The second works even if you have removed all toolbars.

Right-Clicking to Add Toolbars

To display an additional toolbar:

1. Right-click in any non-button area of any visible toolbar.
2. Click the appropriate shortcut menu choice to add any desired toolbar.

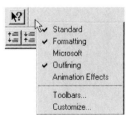

3. The requested toolbar will appear.
4. Repeat steps 1 through 3 to display additional toolbars.

Displaying Toolbars via the View Menu

To display additional toolbars via the View menu, choose Toolbars, then click to place check marks next to the desired toolbars. Click OK.

Moving and Reshaping Toolbars

To change the shape and/or position of a toolbar, simply point to any non-button portion of the toolbar and drag. This will change both the shape and location if you do it right.

Adding Toolbar Buttons

To add or remove toolbar buttons, follow these simple steps:

1. Make sure the toolbar you wish to modify is visible.
2. Choose Customize from the Tools menu.

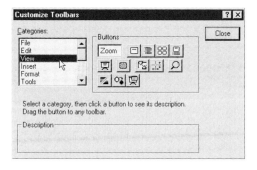

3. Click a category to see the available toolbar buttons. (There is one for each PowerPoint command.)
4. Drag the button of interest to the desired toolbar.
5. When you release the mouse button, the new toolbar button will be inserted.

The Toolbars dialog box also lets you change the size of toolbar buttons. You can also turn off button color here too, if you like, which makes it easier to see the button faces if you have a black-and-white display.

CAUTION

When you remove custom toolbar buttons they are deleted and thus gone forever. Standard buttons, however, are simply removed and not destroyed. Standard buttons can always be restored by using the steps in the "Adding Toolbar Buttons" section.

Removing Toolbar Buttons

1. Make sure the toolbar you wish to modify is visible.
2. Choose Customize from the Tools menu.
3. Drag the button from the toolbar to anyplace else on your screen.

Changing Graphics on Toolbar Button Faces

Whoa, boy gadget freaks. Check this out. You can turn just about any bitmap image into a toolbar button (although small, simple images work best). Since I think you should not waste time doing this, I'll not show you how. But if you must, visit online Help and type **image** in the Find tab, then pick the topics *Change the image on a toolbar button* and *Copy an image from a graphics application to a toolbar button*. Tick tock.

Creating Custom Toolbars

To make your own toolbars, follow these simple steps:

1. Choose Toolbars from the View menu.
2. Choose New.
3. Type the new toolbar's name:

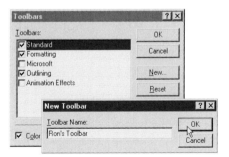

4. Click OK.
5. Visit the Categories list and pick the category or categories containing the desired button(s).
6. Drag the buttons to their new home.
7. Test your work.

Deleting Custom Toolbars

To delete a custom toolbar:

1. Visit the Toolbar choice in the View menu.
2. Select the unwanted toolbar.
3. Click Delete.
4. Click OK.

CUSTOM SPELLING DICTIONARIES

If you want to use more than one custom dictionary (perhaps you are sharing a computer?), follow these steps to select the desired custom spelling dictionary:

1. Make sure that the custom dictionary of your choosing is in the PROOF folder located in the MSAPPS folder, found in the WINDOWS folder (**C:\WINDOWS\MSAPPS\PROOF**).
2. Choose Spelling from the Tools menu, or use the Spelling button on the Standard toolbar. (You won't see the dialog box if there are no misspellings in your presentation.)
3. Choose the desired dictionary from the pop-up list.
4. Click Close.

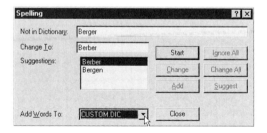

WHAT'S NEXT?

Well, I don't know about you, but after I finish proofing and illustrating this chapter I am going for a walk (and a beer, maybe). Thanks for reading all the way to the end. I hope you enjoyed it. Drop me some e-mail if you have a moment (**rmansfield@aol.com**). Tell me what you liked and what you'd like to see next.

The Basics of
Windows 95

This book assumes that you've already
learned the basics of Windows 95, and have
perhaps read *Windows 95 for Busy People*
(Osborne/McGraw-Hill, 1996). But if you
haven't, this appendix should help you
get started.

All of Microsoft's Office 95 programs (Word, Excel, PowerPoint, Schedule +, and Access) were especially designed to take advantage of the new Windows 95 operating system. If you know your way around Windows 95, you have a leg up on getting the most out of these and many other programs.

THE DESKTOP

Windows 95 starts when you turn on your computer. You don't need to type anything first, but you might be asked for a password once or twice. If you don't know one of the passwords, try pressing the ESC key (you should be able to use Windows but you might not have access to your network or to e-mail; so if passwords are required, you should contact your network administrator to set one up). After Windows 95 starts, it displays a screen called the *desktop*. Figure A.1 shows a typical Windows 95 desktop. Yours might look different. That's perfectly OK.

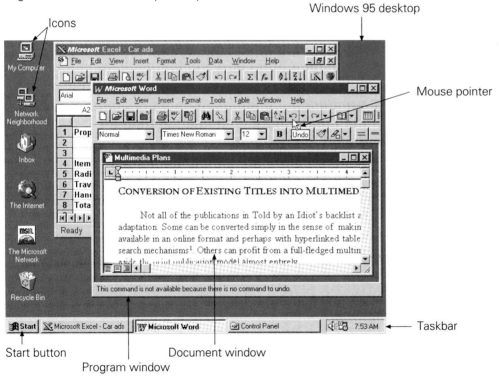

Figure A.1 A typical Windows 95 desktop

The desktop contains small pictures of items like disk drives, a recycle bin, and so on. These little pictures are called *icons*. At the bottom of the Windows 95 desktop you'll probably see the Taskbar, which will be discussed later in this appendix. Windows 95 also displays *windows*. These windows are the spaces in which you do your work. *Program windows* contain programs (like Word, or Excel, or whatever) and can also contain other windows, often called *document windows* or *child windows*. So, for example, you might have a Word window on your desktop with one or more word processing document windows inside it. Any time you double-click a folder icon (or an icon representing a disk drive), it will open up a window on the screen (and a button on the Taskbar), showing the contents of the folder (or drive).

MOUSE BASICS

You use the mouse to point to objects on the desktop. (Incidentally, some computers have trackballs or other pointing devices, but all of these devices share some common characteristics: each has at least two buttons, and each lets you point to things.) As you move the mouse or other pointing device, a corresponding *pointer* moves on the desktop. Sometimes the shape of the pointer changes to give you a clue about what you can do next, because what you can do depends on what you're pointing to.

You can also make choices with the mouse (such as choosing a menu option), and you can use it to move and resize objects. You do this by pointing to something and clicking, which usually selects the object or causes something to happen. *Clicking* is accomplished by pressing and releasing a mouse button. *Double-clicking* is the act of pressing and releasing a mouse button twice in rapid succession. *Dragging* is the act of clicking on an object (a window, an icon, or whatever) and moving your mouse while holding down the button.

Most computer pointing devices (mice, trackballs, and so on) have two buttons. If the buttons are side by side, and if you have not modified Windows 95's default mouse settings, you will use the left button for clicking to select things and initiate most actions. You will also use the left button to drag objects around on the desktop and to change the size and shape of things. (Lefties and others who like to customize their environments can switch the functions of the right and left mouse buttons.)

Windows 95 makes extensive use of the right button as well. Clicking the right button (also called *right-clicking*) on almost any screen element will pop up a *shortcut menu* full of useful options. For example, you can change the appearance of your desktop by right-clicking just about anywhere on the desktop and choosing Properties from the menu that pops up. Many programs, including PowerPoint, will display shortcut menus when you use the right mouse button. Examples of right-clicking appear throughout this book.

There is one more mouse technique worth mentioning. It is called *hovering*. Frequently, if you slide the mouse pointer over an object and leave it there for a second, a little message called a *tool tip* will pop up that will tell you something about the object. In Figure A.1, for example, Word is telling you that the button under the mouse pointer is for activating the Undo feature.

THE TASKBAR

The Taskbar lets you easily run programs and switch from window to window. (If you don't see the Taskbar at the bottom of the desktop, slide your mouse pointer down to the bottom of the screen. The Taskbar should appear.) On the left end of the Taskbar you will always see the Start button. If you have opened windows or started programs (or if Windows has started them for you), your Taskbar will also contain other buttons. See "Taskbar Tips," later, for an explanation of how these buttons work.

The Start Menu

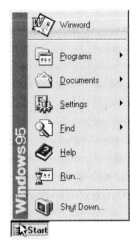

Let's begin with a look at the Start button and the Start menu that is displayed when you click on it. This is the menu from which you start programs, change Windows settings, retrieve recently used documents, find "lost" files, and get Windows 95 help. You point to items in the Start menu to choose them.

Everyone's Start menu looks a little different, particularly when you scratch the surface. (You can also add shortcuts to programs to the Start menu, such as the Winword item at the top of my menu, shown in the illustration here.) The Start menu often reveals additional levels of menus called *submenus*. Let's look at the primary Start menu choices.

Programs

Roughly equivalent to the old Program Manager program groups in earlier versions of Windows, the Programs item on the Start menu pops up a submenu of programs and special Start menu folders. The folders themselves open sub-submenus, and so on. You can run any properly installed program in Windows 95 by clicking on the Start button, then clicking on the Programs choice in the Start menu, and then clicking on the desired program (or perhaps on a folder and then on a program in the folder).

Documents

The Start menu remembers the last 15 documents you've opened and displays their names in the Documents menu. (However, be forewarned that programs designed prior to Windows 95 often fail to add documents to the Documents menu.) When you want to work with a recently used document again, click on its name in the Documents menu. The document will appear on your screen in the program in which it was created. If the program is not already running, Windows 95 will launch it for you automatically

Settings

To change the various settings for your computer, such as the way the Start menu looks or how your screen saver works, choose Settings from the Start menu and then choose Control Panel from the Settings submenu. From the resulting Control Panel window, a part of which is shown here, you can exercise centralized control over all of your computer's settings.

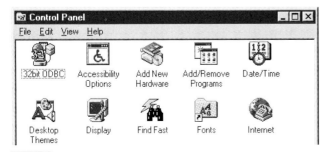

You'll need to consult online help and perhaps read a book like *Windows 95 for Busy People* to learn more about the thousands of possible setting changes.

Find

Windows 95's Find feature can be an invaluable aid for digging up files that seem to be misplaced. To search for a file, choose Find from the Start menu and then choose Files or Folders. In the dialog box that appears, type a filename or part of one in the Named box and press ENTER or click on Find Now.

Help

Stuck? Not sure what to do? You can always consult Windows Help. To do so, choose Help from the Start menu. (If you're doing this for the first time, Windows will tell you that it's setting up Help.) In the Help Topics dialog box that appears (see Figure A.2), click on a topic from the expandable Contents list or click on the Index tab, type a key word in the first box, and choose a topic from the index list in the second box.

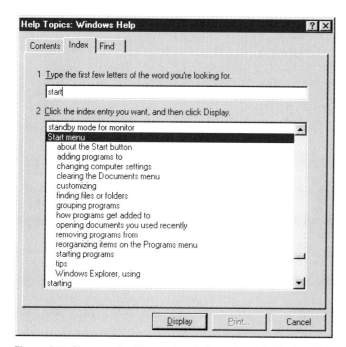

Figure A.2 Choose a topic or subtopic from the Help Topics dialog box

In most programs, if you're not sure what a button or other screen element does, you can hover the mouse pointer over it for a moment and a tool tip will appear, naming or explaining the object.

Also, in a dialog box, you can click on the What's This? button (a question mark) in the top-right corner and then click on the item in the dialog box that you want more information on. A brief explanation should pop up.

Run

Any time you know the name of a program file (although sometimes you also have to know the "path" of the folders on the hard disk that leads to the program), you can choose Run from the Start menu, type the name (or path and name) in the box, and press ENTER to run the program. It's usually easier, though, to start the program from the Start menu or one of its submenus.

Shut Down

When you want to turn off your computer, first shut down Windows 95. To do so, choose Shut Down from the Start menu. Click on Yes when asked if you want to shut down the computer. Wait until Windows tells you it's OK to turn off the computer.

Taskbar Tips

Every time you start a program or open or minimize some types of windows, the program or window gets its own button on the Taskbar.

This makes it easy to switch to a program that is already running, to make a particular window active, or to maximize a window. All you have to do is click on the appropriate button on the Taskbar. When a button looks depressed (pushed in), it means that the task represented by the button is the active one, and its window will appear "in front of" the other windows.

If the Taskbar gets too crowded, you can point to its top edge and drag it so that it gets taller. You can also move the Taskbar to any side of the screen (top, bottom, left, or right) by clicking on any part of the Taskbar that is not a button and dragging. When the Taskbar is on the left or right side, you can drag its inner edge to set it to any width, up to half the width of the screen.

THE MY COMPUTER ICON

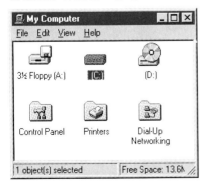

One way to explore the files and programs on your computer is to double-click on the My Computer icon. In general, double-clicking on an icon opens it, runs the program it represents, or runs the program in which the document it represents was created. If the icon is a folder or a special icon such as My Computer, it will open into a window and display its contents, which will also appear as icons. Some of these icons might represent programs, and others might represent folders or other special icons.

The My Computer window contains icons that represent your hard disk drive, floppy disk drives, and CD-ROM drive (if applicable), as well as icons for your printers, the Control Panel, and perhaps for dial-up networking.

Double-click on the hard disk drive icon to see the contents of the hard disk. The icon opens into a window that shows folders and other icons. Double-click on any folder to see its contents. Repeat as often as necessary. You can go back up a folder level by pressing BACKSPACE.

THE NETWORK NEIGHBORHOOD ICON

If your computer is connected to a network, you will see a Network Neighborhood icon on the desktop. Double-clicking on it will show you a list of the remote computers, disk drives, and folders that you can access.

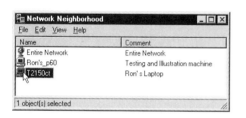

You might need to know the appropriate passwords to access some of the information on the network, and you might be limited in what you can do with files and folders on the network. For example, the owners of some files might let you read the files but not change them. When you have questions, contact your network administrator or help desk.

THE RECYCLE BIN

When you delete files from your hard disk in Windows 95, they are not immediately erased. They are moved to the Recycle Bin. To recover an accidentally deleted file, double-click on the Recycle Bin icon and choose the item or items you wish to restore. Then choose Restore from the File menu in the Recycle Bin window (see Figure A.3).

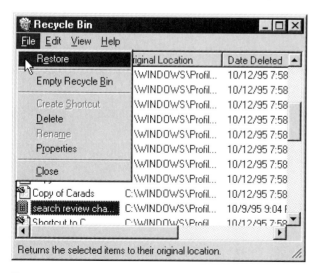

Figure A.3 The Recycle Bin gives you one more chance to "undelete" your files after trashing them

As you add new files to the Recycle Bin, Windows will eventually start discarding the earliest deleted files left. If you want to free up space, right-click on the Recycle Bin and choose Empty Recycle Bin on the File menu.

FOLDERS

You and Windows 95 can organize your files into *folders,* which are the equivalent of directories in oldspeak. You can place folders within folders, thereby creating what used to be called subdirectories. You can create a new folder at any point by right-clicking on the desktop or in a folder (or disk drive) window and choosing New | Folder. You can put a document or program in a folder by dragging its icon onto a folder icon or into an open folder window.

NEW RULES FOR FILENAMES

Windows 95 allows you to use long filenames (up to 255 characters) that include spaces, if you want, so you can give your documents natural sounding names, instead of the pinched, cryptic filenames that DOS used to force on you. Now you can call that document Amortization Projections for 1997 instead of AMTPRJ97.

You might also notice that filename extensions seem to have pretty much disappeared. They're still there at the ends of filenames, but Windows hides all the extensions it recognizes. If you want to see the extensions associated with all filenames, choose Options from the View menu in the My Computer window, the Windows Explorer window, or any folder (or disk drive) window. Click on the View tab. Then uncheck Hide MS-DOS file extensions for file types that are registered. Click on OK. All extensions will appear. To hide most extensions again, repeat the same steps and check the box.

When you are sharing files with non-Windows 95 users, and with programs that were sold prior to the release of Windows 95, filenames get shortened automatically. This can cause some confusion. Again, consult online help and Windows 95 books for details.

WINDOWS EXPLORER

Windows 95 allows you to look through the folders on your computer in a single window, with the entire folder tree in a pane on the left side (sort of like the old File Manager). To do this, choose Programs from the Start menu and Windows Explorer from the Programs menu (or right-click on any folder and choose Explore from the menu that pops up). The Windows Explorer window will appear (see Figure A.4), with its folder tree in the left pane and the contents of the selected folder in the right pane.

To see the contents of a folder, click on it in the left pane. To expand or collapse a folder's contents, double-click on the folder in the left pane (or click the little plus or minus icon in a box to the left of the folder). You can go up a folder level by pressing BACKSPACE, as you can in any such window.

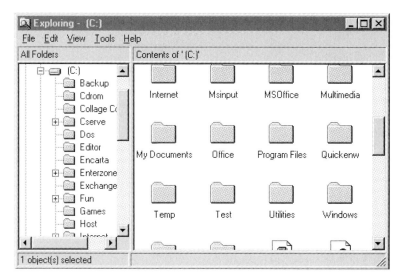

Figure A.4 The Explorer window shows a hierarchical view of the computer in its left pane. There you can thumb through your tree of folders without having to plow through separate folder windows

SHORTCUT ICONS

Windows 95 allows you to create *shortcut icons* that "point to" a program, document, folder, or other Windows 95 resource that you use regularly. This is particularly useful when something you use every day is "buried" in a folder within a folder. A popular place to keep shortcuts is on the desktop. That way, when you want to open your favorite folder, you just double-click on the shortcut icon on the desktop. Another place you can create a shortcut is on the Start menu, where it will look like a normal menu choice, not like a shortcut icon.

In general, the easiest way to create a shortcut is to right-click and drag a copy of the program's icon to the place where you want the shortcut. To do this, open the window that contains the program's original icon. Right-click on the icon and drag to a new location, such as another folder or the desktop. When you release the mouse button, a menu will pop up. Choose Create Shortcut(s) Here to make the shortcut. You'll probably want to rename the new shortcut icon. (Press F2, type a new name, and press ENTER.) If you drag an icon onto the Start button, even without first *right*-clicking, a shortcut to that icon will be placed on the Start menu.

THAT'S THE SHORT COURSE

Well, there you have a taste of Windows 95. Obviously, there's a lot more worth knowing. And the more you learn, the more productive you will become, so I encourage you to do some independent study, either by using Windows 95's online help or by cracking a good book or two.

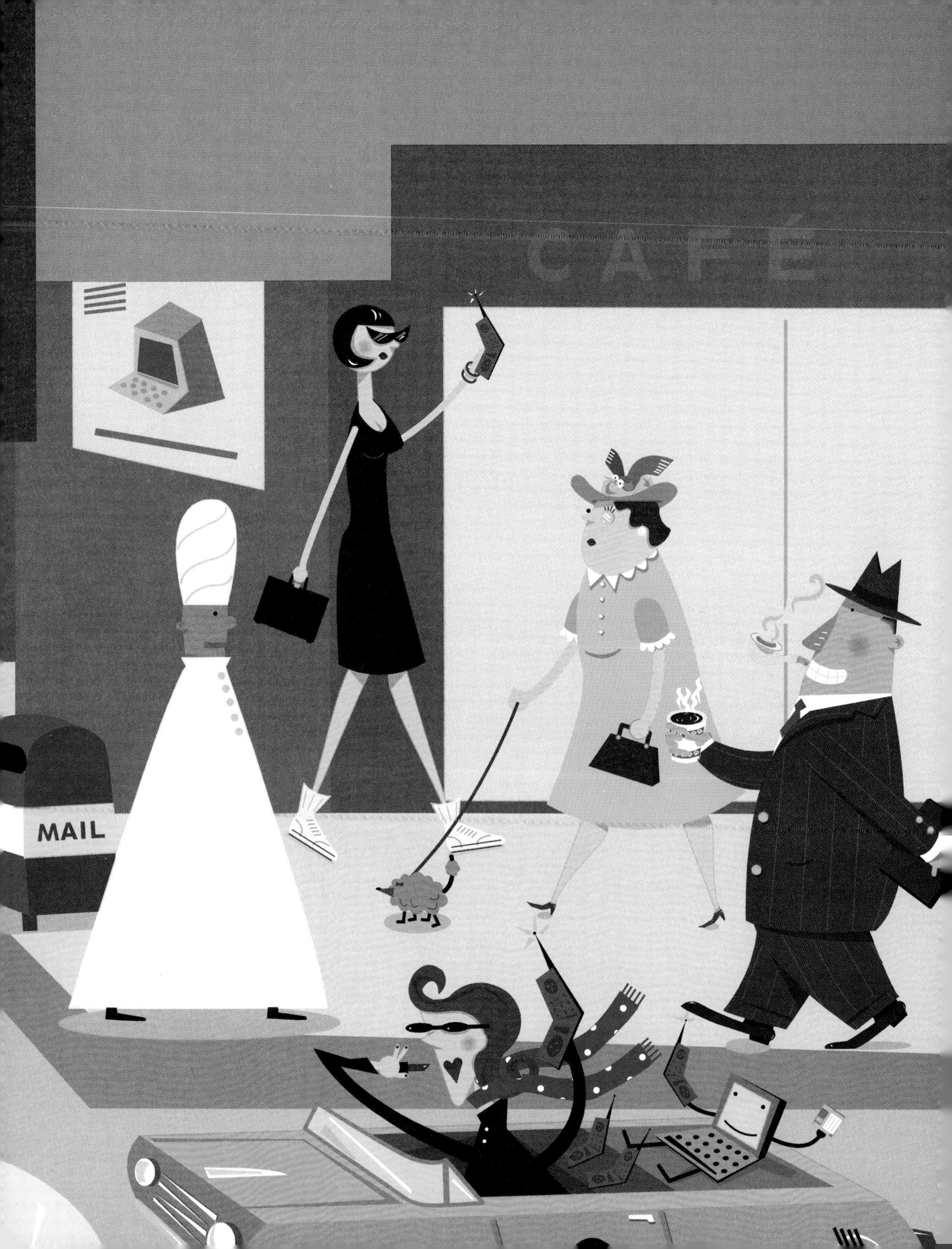
CAFÉ
MAIL

Index

T